Sanctions as Grand Strategy

Brendan Taylor

Sanctions as Grand Strategy

Brendan Taylor

IISS The International Institute for Strategic Studies

The International Institute for Strategic Studies
Arundel House | 13–15 Arundel Street | Temple Place | London | WC2R 3DX | UK

First published May 2010 by **Routledge**
4 Park Square, Milton Park, Abingdon, Oxon, OX14 4RN

for **The International Institute for Strategic Studies**
Arundel House, 13–15 Arundel Street, Temple Place, London, WC2R 3DX, UK
www.iiss.org

Simultaneously published in the USA and Canada by **Routledge**
270 Madison Ave., New York, NY 10016

Routledge is an imprint of Taylor & Francis, an Informa Business

DIRECTOR-GENERAL AND CHIEF EXECUTIVE John Chipman
EDITOR Tim Huxley
MANAGER FOR EDITORIAL SERVICES Ayse Abdullah
ASSISTANT EDITOR Janis Lee
COVER/PRODUCTION John Buck

The International Institute for Strategic Studies is an independent centre for research, information and debate on the problems of conflict, however caused, that have, or potentially have, an important military content. The Council and Staff of the Institute are international and its membership is drawn from almost 100 countries. The Institute is independent and it alone decides what activities to conduct. It owes no allegiance to any government, any group of governments or any political or other organisation. The IISS stresses rigorous research with a forward-looking policy orientation and places particular emphasis on bringing new perspectives to the strategic debate.

The Institute's publications are designed to meet the needs of a wider audience than its own membership and are available on subscription, by mail order and in good bookshops. Further details at www.iiss.org.

Printed and bound in Great Britain by Bell & Bain Ltd, Thornliebank, Glasgow

British Library Cataloguing in Publication Data
A catalogue record for this book is available from the British Library

Library of Congress Cataloging in Publication Data

ADELPHI series
ISSN 1944-5571

ADELPHI 411
ISBN 978-0-415-59529-2

Contents

ACKNOWLEDGEMENTS

A number of friends and colleagues have offered advice and encouragement during the course of this project. In particular, I would like to single out my two dear academic colleagues, Rob Ayson and Bill Tow, who urged me to persist with this book in the face of mounting University teaching and administrative demands. Much appreciation is also due to Jude Blacklock, Paul Dibb, Ralf Emmers, Stephan Fruhling, Greg Fry, Brad Glosserman, Evelyn Goh, Stuart Harris, Ron Huisken, Pauline Kerr, Christine Leah, Jenny Li, Bev Loke, Bill Maley, John Ravenhill, Thu Roberts, Josh Straub, Hannah Taarnby, Shannon Tow, Hugh White and Ping Yu for all of their input and support.

Funding for much of the research upon which this book is based was made available through the Australian Research Council's Centre of Excellence for Policing and Security. Valuable research assistance was provided by Jacob Grooby and Yang Jiang, for which the author is immensely grateful.

A very special note of appreciation is due to Tim Huxley, both for the confidence he has shown in me and for the wonderful editorial support that he has provided at all stages of the project. Tim's input has been absolutely integral to shaping this book and I am confident that it is a much better one as a direct result of his many contributions. Many thanks also to Mark Fitzpatrick, Janis Lee and Adam Ward of the IISS, whose comments on the manuscript were invaluable.

Finally, heartfelt thanks are due to my family, without whom this book simply would not have been written. To my sister Rebecca and her fiancé

Cameron Crouch, thank you for enduring countless conversations related to this project. To my Mum and Dad – Marie and Gerry – I remain forever indebted for all you have done and continue to do for me. Words simply cannot express the depth of my gratitude to you both.

INTRODUCTION

Economic sanctions, an age-old tool of statecraft, are becoming increasingly central to shaping twenty-first-century strategic outcomes. The prominence afforded to economic instruments as part of efforts to address the continuing nuclear crises in Iran and North Korea is but a sign of things to come. The growing centrality of sanctions is partially a reaction to the limits of US military power exposed during difficult and protracted operations in Afghanistan and Iraq. It is symptomatic of the growing number of nuclear or 'near-nuclear' powers in the international system, as epitomised by the Iranian and North Korean cases. More fundamentally, it also reflects a creeping multipolarity stemming from the emergence or re-emergence of centres of power in the forms of China, the European Union (EU), India, Japan and Russia. While armed conflict remains a very real prospect in this environment,[1] the human and financial costs of bringing military forms of coercion to bear in the face of these developments are becoming ever more prohibitive. Both as an alternative to armed force and, conversely, the often cumbersome diplomatic solutions on offer, the salience of sanctions to international security politics is increasingly apparent.

The US, the EU, China, Japan and Russia have all employed sanctions in responding to the Iranian and North Korean nuclear crises. On rare occasions, they have demonstrated some willingness to coordinate their sanctioning strategies.[2] But achieving such coordination and the delicate consensus underpinning it has generally been a painstaking process. These great powers have consistently viewed the use of sanctions quite differently. Moreover, they have invariably favoured sanctions of differing forms and potency when it has come to actually applying these instruments.

The scholarship on sanctions has devoted surprisingly little attention to explaining and understanding these differences in approach. Rather, this voluminous body of work is overwhelmingly US-centric, drawing its conclusions primarily from cases of American sanctions during the Cold War years and into the 1990s (the so-called 'sanctions decade').[3] A substantively lesser, but no less significant body of work analyses sanctions employed through the UN.[4] A handful of studies examine the EU use of sanctions.[5] At least one seminal work also looks at 'middle power' sanctioning strategies, drawing upon the Australian and Canadian experiences as case studies.[6] Beyond these important contributions, however, a study has yet to be produced which compares great-power sanctioning strategies, with a view to ascertaining the distinct ways and conditions under which these actors apply sanctions and the ramifications thereof. By analysing the use of sanctions by the US, the EU, China, Japan and Russia in the context of the Iranian and North Korean nuclear crises, this study proposes to address that shortcoming in the literature.

What are sanctions?

The term 'sanctions' is one of the more confused and confusing to have entered the lexicon and discourse of international politics. Part of the ambiguity surrounding the term stems from the fact that the word 'sanctions' in everyday usage carries multiple meanings. According to the *Oxford Concise Dictionary*, for instance, the term can connote the granting of official permission or approval and, at the same time, a penalty or punishment for disobeying a law or rule. Confusion also results from the tendency of many scholars to use the term 'sanctions' interchangeably with a raft of other descriptors, such as 'economic statecraft', 'economic diplomacy', 'economic coercion', 'economic warfare' and 'economic leverage', to name just a few. Writing in the early 1980s, the political economist Sydney Weintraub suggested that this terminological laxity was of little consequence and that the definition one prefers is largely a matter of 'semantic taste'.[7] Yet a heated debate which unfolded between Kimberly Ann Elliott and Robert Pape on the pages of the prominent academic journal *International Security* more than a decade later clearly suggested otherwise. In this exchange, Pape and Elliott disputed the question of whether sanctions 'work'. Much of their disagreement stemmed from the differing definitions of 'sanctions' that they were each respectively employing. Consistent with this, former US Deputy National Security Adviser on Iraq and Afghanistan Meghan O'Sullivan notes that, 'far from being a semantic debate of no consequence, the definition one adopts determines whether the 1990s are seen as a period of sanctions mayhem or ... one of relative restraint.'[8]

Given this confusion surrounding the term 'sanctions', David Baldwin – the scholar most frequently associated with analysing the use of economic instruments in the service of foreign and security policy objectives – has even gone so far as to suggest that 'there is much to be said for avoiding it altogether'.[9] Yet as Baldwin rightly concedes, because use of the term 'sanctions' has become so deeply embedded – as is the case with many equally problematic, yet inescapably central terms in the international relations vocabulary such as 'terrorism', 'power', 'security' and 'institution' – such a radical course of action is simply not viable.

To avoid adding to the conceptual confusion surrounding the term 'sanctions' and for the purposes of guiding the definition offered here, this study draws upon a taxonomy developed by Baldwin in his classic study *Economic Statecraft*. Firstly, argues Baldwin, in order to qualify for inclusion within this category of statecraft the *type* of policy instrument used has to be economic. Where sanctions are concerned, it is generally assumed that trade (including travel and arms sales) and/or financial measures are involved.[10] Secondly, the *domain* of the influence attempt is usually another, or more than one, international actor. While the nation state was still widely regarded as the primary unit of analysis in international politics when Baldwin first developed his schema, it is generally now taken for granted that significant non-state actors – such as transnational criminal syndicates and terrorist groups – can also be the target of such influence attempts. The final component of Baldwin's framework is the *scope* of the influence attempt, which ought to encompass some dimension of that entity's behaviour (including its beliefs, attitudes, opinions, expectations, emotions and propensities to act). Following this approach, for the purposes of this study a sanction will be defined as 'an economic instrument which is employed by one or more international actors against another, ostensibly with a view to influencing that entity's foreign and/or security policy behaviour.'

Addressing scholarly shortcomings

The Iranian and North Korean nuclear crises present suitable comparative case studies for a project of this nature. They each share a number of important similarities. Both are high profile cases exhibiting a commensurate degree of contemporary salience. They revolve around the nuclear programmes of two so-called 'rogue' states that have attracted a high level of international abhorrence and condemnation. Yet they are both 'hard' cases in terms of the capacity of external pressure to alter the policies of Pyongyang and Tehran, particularly given that the North Korean and Iranian nuclear programmes have assumed such importance in the strategic thinking and domestic politics of the two regimes. Both cases appear to entail the use of sanctions for clear-cut instrumental, strategic purposes. In other words, sanctions are not ostensibly employed merely for symbolic or expressive purposes in either case. The two cases are also inter-related in important ways. Over recent years, the increasing level of cooperation between Iran and North Korea in the area of ballistic missile technology has become a matter of growing international concern. Finally, the course of these two nuclear crises carries important regional (for the Middle East in the case of Iran and for Northeast Asia in the case of North Korea) and global security ramifications. All of the great powers considered in this study thus have a keen interest in how these two nuclear crises ultimately play out.

To facilitate comparison of the sanctioning strategies of these great powers across the two case studies, the following sequence of questions is asked. *How have the US, the EU, China, Japan and Russia employed sanctions differently in each of the cases?* Consideration here will be given to the use of sanctions by these great powers both in multilateral settings – for example, in a UN context or within ad hoc coalitions – and, as applicable, the unilateral employment of these instruments. Emphasis will also be given to the particular forms of sanction – for example, financial restrictions, travel bans or arms embargos – that each of the great powers has tended to favour. Such an approach is novel given that sanctions scholars rarely seek to differentiate between various forms of sanction – beyond, that is, the setting up of relatively crude and imprecise dichotomies between, for example, 'comprehensive' and 'selective' or 'smart' measures – when assessing the utility of these instruments. Consideration will also be given to the relative potency of the sanction in question. Most notably in the multilateral context, particular focus will be directed towards the question of whether sanctions that were ultimately applied were implemented in a manner consistent with their initial conception. Or conversely, did great-power bargaining over the decision to employ sanctions lead to a dilution of the instrument? Finally, the analysis of *how* the great powers have employed sanctions differently will also take into account the balance between sanctions and incentives – or in common parlance 'carrots' and 'sticks' – in the sanctioning strategies of these actors.

When and why have the US, the EU, China, Japan and Russia used sanctions differently in responding to the Iranian and North Korean nuclear crises? Consideration will be given here to the range of factors that can profoundly shape the nature and scope of sanctions employed. Did the great powers in question exhibit a more general proclivity towards or aversion to the use of sanctions based, for instance, on their material circumstances or their previous experiences involving the use of these instruments? What is the nature of the relationship that each of these great powers shares with Iran and North Korea and what conditioning influence has this had upon their willingness and ability to use sanctions against these two so-called 'rogue states'? Have the regimes in Tehran and Pyongyang actually even been the primary targets of the great-power sanctions in question?

Finally, *how 'effectively' have the US, the EU, China, Japan and Russia used economic sanctions and what factors have conditioned the 'effectiveness' of their sanctioning strategies?* The issue of sanctions 'efficacy' is a notoriously slippery one. On that issue, this study takes a broader view of 'efficacy' than that traditionally adopted by sanctions scholars. While acknowledging, as the vast majority of sanctions scholarship assumes, that influencing the policies of a target actor can certainly constitute one measure of 'success', sanctions may also be used to fulfill domestic political objectives. Only a handful of sanctions scholars consciously acknowledge that possibility. Even fewer, however, go as far as this study does in also considering the extent to which the use of these instruments contributes towards meeting the broader grand strategic aims and objectives of the great powers.

Argument in brief

Great powers do not use sanctions merely for the purpose of influencing the behaviour of a publicly designated 'target' actor. Nor do they typically invoke them solely for largely symbolic reasons, such as expressing disdain internationally or deflecting pressures emanating from within their own domestic constituencies. Rather, this book argues that such considerations are not foremost in the minds of great-power policymakers when they opt to employ these instruments. Instead, the major contention of this study is that, while great-power policymakers will typically invoke sanctions with the stated aim of coercing a publicly designated 'target' actor, their actual goal is often to influence one another in the context of executing and advancing their respective grand strategies. The great-power posturing and bargaining processes which ensue, it is argued here, often result in a significant 'watering down' of the sanctions measures in question, thereby considerably diminishing their capacity to inflict pain and suffering upon the publicly designated 'target' actor. This is one of the key reasons why sanctions scholars so often find that these instruments simply don't 'work' in terms of meeting their purported aims.

That said, the utility of sanctions in the context of the grand strategic game between nations explains why great-power policymakers continue to exhibit such a strong propensity towards employing these instruments. Taken together, this line of argument thus offers a promising solution to the longstanding and as yet unresolved sanctions paradox of 'why do policymakers continue to invoke these instruments despite their seemingly limited capacity to influence "target" actor policies and behaviours?'

CHAPTER ONE

The Sanctions Debate

The centrality of sanctions in two of the most pressing diplomatic crises of our time – the Iranian and North Korean nuclear crises – is by no means a historical anomaly. Through the centuries, sanctions have been prominent in many of history's most pivotal moments. Thucydides' classic history of the Peloponnesian War, for instance, describes a trade boycott imposed by Athens on Sparta's ally Megara in 432 BCE, which was widely believed to have caused the Peloponnesian War.[1] By contrast, following the conclusion of the First World War US President Woodrow Wilson reflected a sense of optimism regarding the use of sanctions when he described them as a 'peaceful, silent, deadly remedy', the application of which would mean that 'there will be no need for force'.[2] Sanctions were once again at the centre of the second catastrophic conflict of the twentieth century; the US fuel and steel embargo on Japan is widely viewed as motivating the latter's December 1941 attack on Pearl Harbor.[3] More recently, the perceived failure of comprehensive sanctions against Iraq during the 1990s was a central component of neo-conservative arguments as to why unilateral military force needed to be applied against Saddam

Hussein's regime in March 2003.[4] Outlining the Bush administration's case for removing Saddam in a speech delivered in
August 2002, Vice President Dick Cheney referred specifically
to the failure of UN sanctions: 'Saddam has perfected the game
of shoot and retreat, and is very skilled in the art of denial and
deception. A return of inspectors would provide no assurance
whatsoever of his compliance with UN resolutions.'[5]

Sanctions only became the subject of serious empirical
inquiry, however, in the 1960s. During the period since, sanctions scholars have been preoccupied with the question of
whether these instruments of statecraft actually 'work'. Much
of the ink which has been spilled in seeking an answer to this
question has found in the negative. This, in turn, led to the
emergence of the so-called sanctions paradox of 'why, given
their apparently dubious utility, do policymakers continue to
apply these instruments with such frequency?' Three competing schools of thought have emerged seeking to account for
this puzzle. The first – which I term the 'sanctions don't work'
school – denigrates outright the utility of these instruments and
attributes their continued application to 'foolish' misjudgement
on the part of policymakers. The second 'sanctions as symbols'
school posits that these instruments perform a range of useful
'expressive' functions that are quite separate from influencing
the behaviour of the actor against which they are ostensibly
targeted. The third 'sanctions can work' school suggests that
sanctions are not inherently flawed, but that they can be effective provided that policymakers wield them properly.

The 'sanctions don't work' school

The earliest systematic analysis of sanctions came in the
form of Norwegian sociologist Johan Galtung's study of
UN-mandated sanctions against Rhodesia in response to that
country's 1965 Unilateral Declaration of Independence from

the United Kingdom. Galtung's study presented a disparaging assessment of sanctions, concluding: 'the probable effective-ness of economic sanctions is, generally, negative.'[6] He offered a number of possible rationales for why 'sanctions don't work'. First and foremost, he said, they often create a 'rally round the flag' effect wherein support for the ruling regime in the target country actually increases in the face of external pressure. What Galtung was suggesting is that the economic deprivation resulting from sanctions can exact a politically integrative – as opposed to a disintegrative – effect in the target state, contrary to the logic regarding how these instruments are ideally designed to work.

Further undermining the efficacy of sanctions, in Galtung's view, were the difficulties associated with obtaining the universal application of these measures. These difficulties were created both by the unwillingness of some countries to participate and by the capacity of the target to circumvent the sanctions through, for example, obtaining access to prohibited goods and services via the black market or third-party suppli-ers. Galtung also pointed to a range of other counter-measures that countries could take to immunise themselves against sanc-tions measures. They could, for instance, diversify their national economy to decrease their reliance upon certain exports, thereby lessening their vulnerability to sanctions measures targeting a small number of key exports. Likewise, nations could diversify their trading relationships to avoid becoming unduly depen-dent upon one source of imports. Finally, Galtung also argued that 'sanctions don't work' on the grounds that target actors can work towards becoming economically and politically self-sufficient as a classic countermeasure against the imposition of sanctions.[7]

Galtung's assessment set the tone for the voluminous body of scholarship which was to emerge over the subsequent few decades. While, as this chapter goes on to demonstrate, contributions to this literature have not provided uniformly negative assessments of the economic instrument, the view that 'sanctions don't work' remains dominant.[8] Most scholars associated with this school of thought have tended to base their negative assessments of sanctions upon the finding that these instruments were unable to visibly influence the policies of the leadership against which they were ostensibly targeted.

The 'sanctions as symbols' school

The 'sanctions as symbols' school also owes an intellectual debt to the work of Galtung. Although Galtung argued that sanctions were generally ineffectual in terms of fulfilling the *instrumental* purpose of eliciting compliance from the target actor, he also observed that sanctions could perform a range of useful symbolic or 'expressive' functions. In Galtung's terms: 'When military action is impossible for one reason or another, and when doing nothing is seen as tantamount to complicity, then *something has to be done to express morality*, something that at least serves as a clear signal to everyone that what the receiving nation has done is disapproved of.'[9] In this regard, he saw sanctions as a tool for expressing and reinforcing international morality.

The range of 'expressive' purposes to which sanctions may be put is amorphous and, hence, symbolism as a sanctions objective potentially lacks analytical meaning and utility.[10] To negotiate this difficulty, when contemplating the symbolic utility of these instruments scholars have tended to think of sanctions in terms of two further analytical subcategories: *international* symbolism and *domestic* symbolism. Where *international* symbolism is concerned the target audience is the wider international community. For great powers, sanctions employed for *international* symbolic purposes are especially pertinent given the normative duties attached to great-powerhood, such as the duty to be seen to be acting 'responsibly' in providing and maintaining order.[11] Sanctions imposed for *domestic* symbolic purposes, by contrast, are often applied with a view to placating powerful domestic constituencies calling from within for decisive action in response to the policies or behaviour of the target. Similarly, the leadership of the sender state might also use sanctions to *symbolise* its resolve in the face of domestic criticism regarding the inadequacy of its foreign policy approach vis-à-vis that target. It goes without saying here, of course, that any *domestic* symbolic functions of sanctions will likely exhibit far greater salience to the democratic actors examined in this study than to their authoritarian counterparts.

The 'sanctions can work' school

While the view that sanctions are inherently ineffective tools of statecraft remains dominant, several waves of scholarship have emerged seeking to challenge this line of thinking through making the case that sanctions can indeed 'work' in terms of influencing the policies of the actor against which they are ostensibly targeted. The roots of this 'sanctions can work' school can be dated back to the interwar years, reflecting the high level of optimism that existed among practitioners at that time regarding the efficacy of sanctions. Arguably the most famous scholarly exposition of this view was put forward by political theorist David Mitrany, who in his 1925 study of sanctions asserted that 'the economic weapon is at present the only one generally available for the enforcement of peace.'[12] Despite its historical significance, however, pioneering efforts such as Mitrany's cannot be regarded as serious empirical endeavours, at least when measured against the methodological demands of modern social science.

The first genuinely rigorous body of scholarship positing that 'sanctions can work' appeared in the early 1980s with the release of a monograph by three scholars – Gary Clyde Hufbauer, Jeffrey J. Schott and Kimberly Ann Elliott – whose names remain at the very forefront of sanctions research. Their study challenged the dominant paradigm that 'sanctions don't work' by producing data to suggest that these instruments are effective approximately 30% of the time, provided that the economic and political conditions in the target state are susceptible to their influence and depending upon the nature of the goals sought by the sender. But most importantly, sanctions could be even more effective if they were implemented properly. To this end, Hufbauer, Schott and Elliott provided 'nine commandments' for the effective use of sanctions.[13] These guidelines were further developed and refined in their 1985 landmark study *Economic Sanctions Reconsidered*, which was based upon the analysis of 103 sanctions episodes.[14]

Building on this work, a growing number of scholars by the late 1990s were arguing that sanctions could indeed 'work' and that the primary reason for their mixed record of success lay in the fact that policymakers were generally 'fools' who simply could not apply them optimally.[15] Works belonging to this second wave of 'sanctions can work' scholarship identified a wide range of variables claimed to condition sanctions effectiveness including the length of time these measures are applied; the size differential and the trade and security linkages between the sender and target; whether the sanctions are threatened or actually applied; the political economy of the target and the domestic political situation in the sender state; and the level of international cooperation involved in implementing the sanctions measures.[16]

Most recently, a third body of scholarship has emerged arguing that 'sanctions can work', provided that they are appropriately targeted. Following this logic, a new category of selective measures known as 'smart sanctions' was first recognised in the 1990s. Its appeal among scholars and practitioners alike grew over the past decade. As alluded to previously, 'smart sanctions' are typically juxtaposed with 'general' or 'comprehensive' sanctions. The latter are regarded as inherently 'blunter' instruments by virtue of the fact that they don't specifically target the leadership whose policies the sender is trying to influence and tend, instead, to inflict pain and suffering upon the population of the target country more generally. This outcome is seen as undesirable in that it weakens opposition to the incumbent leadership of the target, thereby potentially creating Galtung's 'rally round the flag' effect. 'Smart sanctions' are designed to avoid these outcomes by applying 'maximum pressure on the culpable actors while at the same time minimising the adverse humanitarian impacts'.[17] A carefully calibrated arms embargo, for example, can limit the capacity of the ruling regime in the target country to initiative military action, either externally or against its own citizens. US Assistant Secretary of State for Verification and Compliance Rose Gottemoeller, who negotiated the successor to the 1991 Strategic Arms Reduction Treaty (START-1, signed in April 2010), perhaps best captured the sense of optimism surrounding this latest variant of the 'sanctions can work' school. She observed on the pages of *Survival* that 'the concept of smart sanctions introduced after the humanitarian crisis in Iraq in the 1990s has been honed through the "war on terror", and sanctions are hitting their targets among corrupt elites more often'.[18]

Summing up the sanctions debate

The 'sanctions paradox' remains unresolved. None of the three schools discussed in this chapter has emerged uncontested through its capacity to provide an unequivocal answer to the puzzle of why policymakers continue to employ these instruments. This study is premised upon two underlying assumptions as to why sanctions scholars have, thus far, been unable to satisfactorily address this conundrum. The first relates to the relatively narrow manner in which sanctions cases have been selected and studied. The vast majority of sanctions studies have drawn their conclusions from cases involving the US and, to a lesser extent, UN use of these instruments. This focus is certainly understandable, given that these two actors have been the most frequent users of these instruments. As other great powers also increasingly employ sanctions – both unilaterally and in multilateral settings – it now seems appropriate to broaden that focus to compare their invocations of sanctions with those of the US and the UN. Secondly, this study proceeds from the assumption that sanctions scholars continue to cling far too tightly to identifying changes in target behaviour and policies as the primary criterion for determining whether the use of these instruments succeeds. By arguing that great powers employ sanctions not only to influence 'target' actor behaviour – and (in some cases) as instruments geared towards the expression of international or domestic symbolism – but also one another in the context of the larger grand -strategic games that nations notoriously play, this study hopes to circumvent that shortcoming in the sanctions literature and aspires, in the process, to shed much-needed light upon the so-called 'sanctions paradox'.

CHAPTER TWO

Sanctioning North Korea

The North Korean nuclear crisis has at the time of writing reached an impasse. The Six-Party Talks – the diplomatic process comprising the US, North Korea, South Korea, China, Japan and Russia designed specifically to address this crisis – have not convened since September 2007. North Korea officially withdrew from these talks in April 2009. Sanctions can be seen both as part of the problem and as part of a potential solution to the present impasse. Until North Korea takes 'concrete measures' towards denuclearisation and agrees to return to the talks, the other five members – ostensibly at least – maintain they will not lift sanctions imposed against it, most recently following its nuclear test of May 2009. In a manifestation of those sanctions, the Thai authorities in December 2009 seized 35 tonnes of weaponry (including rocket-propelled grenades and missiles) sourced from North Korea and bound for an unspecified location in South Asia or the Middle East from a cargo plane refuelling in Bangkok.[1] A similar seizure took place in August 2009, when authorities from the United Arab Emirates (UAE) intercepted ten containers of North Korean military hardware from an Australian-owned vessel bound for Iran.[2]

North Korea flatly refuses to return to the Six-Party Talks until UN sanctions imposed against it are lifted and a peace treaty with the US is signed to formally end the 1950–53 Korean War. Pyongyang regards the removal of UN sanctions, in particular, as an essential 'confidence building measure'.[3] Interestingly, Pyongyang has not proven averse to threatening diplomatic sanctions of its own, asserting in January 2010 that it would cease all dialogue with South Korea and exclude it from future negotiations regarding the security of the Korean Peninsula following reports that Seoul had updated a contingency plan for responding to internal unrest in North Korea.[4]

That said, there is little evidence to suggest that sanctions are significantly influencing Pyongyang's decision-making calculus. The seizures of North Korean arms by Thai and UAE authorities, for instance, constituted only a small fraction of the estimated 'hundreds of millions of dollars' which Pyongyang earns each year from illegal arms exports.[5] Yet there are also indications that sanctions could well be causing the humanitarian situation in North Korea to deteriorate significantly. Recent reports suggest that cuts in food aid and shipments of fertiliser by South Korea and the US are deepening North Korea's already dire humanitarian crisis.[6] If sanctions appear to be having minimal impact upon Pyongyang's calculations and if their continued application is proving potentially destabilising, why then have great power policymakers persisted in supporting their usage in the context of the North Korean nuclear crisis?

Background

Sanctions have long had a prominent place as part of international efforts to address the vexing and protracted North Korean nuclear problem. At the height of the 1993–94 North Korean nuclear crisis, for instance, the US Ambassador to the UN,

Madeleine Albright, announced that preparations had begun on a draft sanctions resolution which the UK, France and Russia were willing to co-sponsor. Pyongyang responded aggressively to such suggestions, threatening that any international attempt to impose sanctions against it would be regarded as a 'declaration of war', the advent of which would result in South Korea's capital Seoul being turned 'into a sea of fire'.[7] Despite this, the US, Japan and South Korea continued to contemplate the application of limited sanctions against North Korea at various times throughout the 1993–94 nuclear crisis.[8] Moreover, the 1994 Agreed Framework which provided a temporary solution to that earlier crisis has been frequently characterised as a 'positive sanction', in that it offered Pyongyang a series of economic, technological and political incentives in return for the dismantlement of its nuclear programme.[9] Under the terms of that agreement, Washington was also to undertake a broad easing of American sanctions against North Korea.

The Agreed Framework essentially collapsed following a visit to Pyongyang in October 2002 by US Assistant Secretary of State James Kelly. During this visit, Kelly confronted his North Korean counterparts, asserting that the US had evidence that Pyongyang was continuing to secretly develop nuclear weapons using uranium-enrichment technology, thereby contravening the terms of the 1994 Agreed Framework. The Agreed Framework subsequently broke down when the US stopped the provision of fuel oil and North Korea responded by expelling International Atomic Energy Agency (IAEA) inspectors.

A new diplomatic avenue for resolving the North Korean nuclear problem opened up in 2003, however, with the establishment of the Six-Party Talks. This process has enjoyed a relatively mixed record, enjoying some limited successes – such as arriving at agreement in September 2005 on a 'roadmap' for resolving the crisis – but stalling on numerous occasions and, indeed, for lengthy periods.

The latest manifestation of the North Korean nuclear crisis which provides the focus for this chapter began to intensify in July 2006 after Pyongyang test-fired seven missiles, including an intermediate-range *Taepo-dong*-2 ballistic missile similar to that which sparked an international crisis in August 1998 when the North test-fired one over Japan. The current crisis deepened still further in October 2006, when North Korea conducted its first nuclear test. Because the test yield was less than one kiloton, there has been much speculation that it was technically a fizzle, although with large political ramifications. As this chapter goes on to detail, sanctions formed a central component of the international response to North Korea's nuclear and missile tests in 2006. A similar pattern of events unfolded in 2009, leading to a further deepening of the North Korean crisis. In April of that year, Pyongyang conducted a rocket launch which it claimed was undertaken to put a satellite into orbit, but which most international commentators contend was a ruse designed to disguise a second North Korean test of the *Taepo-dong*-2. Less ambiguity surrounded Pyongyang's second major provocation of 2009, when on 25 May 2009 a second, apparently more successful underground nuclear test was conducted.

In response to these developments, the United Nations Security Council (UNSC) has passed three key resolutions containing sanctions pertaining specifically to North Korea. The first of these – UNSC Resolution 1695 – was passed on 15 July 2006. Resolution 1695 'condemned' these tests, 'demanded' that North Korea suspend its ballistic-missile programme (thus returning to its previously agreed-upon moratorium on missile launching), and 'urged' Pyongyang to 'return immediately' to the Six-Party Talks. Broadly speaking, two forms of sanction were included in UNSCR 1695. Firstly, UN member states were required to prevent the procurement and transfer of 'missile or missile-related items, materials, goods and technology' to and from North Korea. Second, UNSCR 1695 also called upon UN member states to prevent the transfer of 'financial resources in relation to [North Korea's] missiles or WMD programmes'.[10] One respected analyst has recently characterised these sanctions as 'the strongest reprimand of North Korea by the Security Council since 1950', while suggesting also that these measures 'clearly represented an escalating response on the part of the UN'.[11]

Sanctions of increasing stringency once again formed a central element of the international response to the North Korean nuclear test of 9 October 2006. The Security Council moved swiftly on this occasion, passing Resolution 1718 only five days following the North's nuclear test. This resolution banned the trade of items related to North Korea's weapons of mass destruction programmes, including heavy military equipment (tanks, ballistic missiles, jet fighters and ships), dual-use items and luxury goods. It required all member states to freeze the funds and financial assets of those individuals (and entities) associated with the North's weapons programmes, while also prohibiting these individuals from travelling abroad.

Finally, in a move which arguably formalised the US-led Proliferation Security Initiative (PSI) – a multilateral export-control initiative designed to prevent the transfer of weapons of mass destruction, their delivery systems and related materials[12] – UNSCR 1718 also authorised and encouraged UN member states to inspect North Korean vessels suspected of carrying illicit weapons material.[13] The Security Council subsequently reaffirmed UNSCR 1718 and agreed to adjust the terms of this resolution by explicitly designating the entities and goods to face sanctions following the North Korean rocket launch of April 2009.[14]

No new resolution was passed in response to the April 2009 North Korean rocket launch, primarily because the UNSC could not reach agreement to do so. Such was not the case following the North Korean nuclear test of May 2009, however, to which the UNSC responded by imposing a third resolution containing sanctions targeting Pyongyang. Resolution 1874 was passed on 12 June 2009, almost three weeks following the North's 25 May 2009 nuclear test. More than two weeks of this period was taken up by intensive negotiations between the permanent five members of the Security Council, in conjunction with Japan and South Korea. The resulting resolution built upon the previous UNSC measures, adding four new sanctions. Firstly, the prohibition on North Korean exports of heavy military equipment contained in Resolution 1718 was extended to all arms, while member states were prohibited from selling arms – with the exception of small arms or light arms – to North Korea. Resolution 1874 required member states to 'exercise vigilance' over small arms or light weapons transfers and to inform the UNSC at least five days prior to engaging in such transactions. Secondly, Resolution 1874 authorised all member states to inspect suspicious North Korean vessels on the high seas, provided that the prior consent of that vessel's flag state was obtained. In situations where that consent was not forthcoming, the resolution required the flag state in question to re-direct the vessel to a nearby port, where an inspection would then be conducted by local authorities. Thirdly, all member states and financial institutions were required to suspend financial assistance, loans and export credits to North Korea, with the exception of those intended for 'humanitarian and developmental purposes'. Finally, UNSCR 1874 also called upon member states to cease the specialised training of North Korean nationals which could assist Pyongyang's nuclear-weapons programmes.[15]

US sanctions

The US was a strong supporter and, in most cases, a prime mover behind each of the three aforementioned UNSC resolutions. Such support is entirely consistent with the American use of sanctions against North Korea, which dates back approximately six decades. Dianne Rennack – a sanctions expert at the Congressional Research Service – suggests that the US has generally justified using unilateral sanctions against North Korea because the North constitutes a threat to US national security. Elaborating on this overarching justification, she explains that US sanctions have been rationalised on at least one of three grounds: North Korea's previous sponsorship of terrorist organisations, its status as a Marxist–Leninist state with a Communist government, and on the basis of evidence pointing to Pyongyang's involvement in nuclear-proliferation activities.[16]

At the opening of the Korean War in June 1950, for example, the US introduced an embargo on all exports to North Korea. While most of these restrictions were eased in the years following the cessation of hostilities, further US sanctions against the North were imposed throughout the Cold War. When the US Department of Commerce revised its Export Administration regulations in 1965, for instance, North Korea was placed on its most restricted list. Following the bombing of Korean Air Lines flight 858 in 1987, North Korea was also added to the US Department of State's list of countries considered to be state sponsors or supporters of international terrorism, leading to further trade and financial restrictions. Throughout the 1990s, however, a number of US sanctions against North Korea were lifted in the context of improving bilateral relations between

Washington and Pyongyang and, specifically, in support of President Bill Clinton's policy of engagement with the North. Sanctions pertaining to the export of goods from the US commercial sector, for example, were relaxed for those cases where American exports were addressing 'basic human needs'. As alluded to earlier, a further easing of US sanctions against North Korea constituted part of the 1994 Agreed Framework. In 2000, the Clinton administration subsequently eased sanctions against the North to allow for the trade of most goods for civilian use, while also significantly relaxing US sanctions on travel. These steps were a direct result of Pyongyang's agreement to implement a moratorium on missile testing.[17]

In line with this history – and in addition to the leading role that Washington has played in seeking to introduce new sanctions resolutions through the UNSC – the use of sanctions (both in terms of the application and the relaxation of these instruments) has formed a central element of America's response to the most recent manifestation of the North Korean nuclear crisis. During this crisis, Washington has increasingly favoured the use of selective financial measures, premised largely upon the logic that these instruments are more discriminate in terms of their capacity to target members of the North Korean leadership and their affiliates with direct responsibility for supporting Pyongyang's nuclear and missile programmes, while avoiding the infliction of further pain and suffering upon the North Korean population more generally. Further, this is seen as playing to America's strength as the world's leading financial centre.

By far the most famous and controversial US financial sanction during this period was that targeting a Macau-based bank named Banco Delta Asia. In September 2005, using authority provided by the Patriot Act of 2001, the US Treasury Department identified Banco Delta Asia as a 'financial institution of primary money laundering "concern"'. Notwithstanding denials from the bank's representatives, this designation caused a run on the bank by depositors which led Macau authorities to seize control of Banco Delta Asia, freeze suspect North Korean accounts worth a total value of $24 million, and begin conducting an audit. While the amount of funds frozen was relatively small, this action had wider repercussions in making banks around the world less willing to deal with North Korea. Moreover, the case also carried greater importance than the monetary amount alone, given that at least some of the funds apparently belonged personally to the North Korea leader Kim Jong-il. The funds were eventually released to a Russian bank as part of a US-led deal to lift the Banco Delta Asia sanction.

The US has applied financial sanctions more directly against a range of other entities around the world as part of its efforts to thwart North Korean nuclear ambitions. In March 2006, for instance, the US Treasury Department froze the assets of a Swiss company and banned US companies from doing business with that company on the grounds that it had commercial ties with a sanctioned North Korean firm.[18] Similarly, in July 2009 the US froze the assets of the Namchongang Trading Company for its alleged involvement in Pyongyang's nuclear programmes. This Pyongyang-based company was sanctioned based on evidence that it had been involved in the purchase of aluminium tubes and other equipment related to North Korea's uranium-enrichment programme, as well as for its suspected complicity in North Korean assistance for Syria's nuclear programme.[19]

The US has also continued to use the 'lifting' of existing sanctions with a view to influencing the course of the North Korean nuclear crisis. The March 2007 decision to facilitate the release of $24m in North Korean accounts held at Banco Delta Asia, for instance, provides one prominent example of this technique. Taking further the aforementioned lifting of sanctions that the Clinton administration initiated in September 2000 after Pyongyang's agreement to a missile moratorium, President George W. Bush in June 2008 agreed to lift the sanctions imposed under the Trading with the Enemy Act to remove North Korea from the US state sponsors of terrorism list.[20] Inclusion on the list incurs a range of sanctions, including prohibitions on the US export of items that could be used for both civilian and military purposes (dual-use items), as well as defence exports and sales. Perhaps more significantly from Pyongyang's perspective, inclusion on the state sponsors of terrorism list also entailed US opposition to assistance for North Korea from international financial institutions such as the World Bank and the International Monetary fund. The removal of North Korea from this list, along with the lifting of Trading with the Enemy Act-based sanctions, was subsequently completed in October 2008.[21]

To be sure, in recent years US sanctions have increasingly homed in on the Kim Jong-il regime in the context of the North Korean nuclear crisis. The US has employed targeted instruments not only with a view to punishing Pyongyang for its recalcitrant behaviour, but also in an effort to influence the decision-making calculus of the North Korean leadership. Some officials within the Bush administration reportedly even entertained the idea of producing 'regime change' through the use of sanctions.[22] American sanctions were also employed with a view to facilitating a diplomatic solution to the North Korea nuclear crisis through supporting the Six-Party Talks. During periods when these talks had stalled, sanctions were imposed in an attempt to coerce North Korea back to the table; or, conversely, some measures were lifted with the intention of kick-starting talks.

Beyond the goal of seeking to influence the decision-making calculus in Pyongyang, two other broad objectives have underpinned the US use of sanctions vis-à-vis North Korea. Firstly, American sanctions have been employed in the service of domestic political objectives. The Bush administration, for instance, struggled to resolve a persistent and at times intense internal debate over North Korea policy. On one side stood moderates from the State Department – headed by lead negotiator in the Six-Party Talks Christopher Hill – who favoured engagement with the North and saw the diplomatic route as the most likely means of achieving a lasting solution to the difficult and protracted North Korean nuclear crisis. On the other side, a group of 'hardliners' – which included such prominent players as the office of Vice President Dick Cheney and Undersecretary of State for Arms Control John Bolton, and his successor Robert Joseph – called for a tougher approach and believed the only viable route to solving the North Korean crisis was through changing the regime in Pyongyang.[23] Sanctions offered a useful 'middle way' between these two competing groups, catering somewhat to the preferences of the latter while simultaneously allowing the diplomatic route advocated by the moderates to continue. State Department officials realised that the Banco Delta Asia sanctions could jeopardise the Six-Party Talks, but there was overwhelming governmental support for employing financial leverage to punish North Korean currency counterfeiting and other economic crimes.

Secondly, the US has also used sanctions in the context of the North Korean nuclear crisis with a view to influencing a range of third parties. Both via the leading role that it has played in initiating and supporting the application of sanctions through the UN, as well as through its unilateral application of sanctions, the US has sought to send a message of deterrence to foreign governments who might consider heading down the same nuclear path as Pyongyang. From Washington's perspective, the fact that so many countries – including China, Russia and South Korea, each of whom had traditionally opposed the use of such measures against North Korea – were willing to sign up to UN sanctions was highly positive. US policymakers saw this 'unprecedented' level of support for sanctions as conveying a very strong symbolic message, not only to the leadership in Pyongyang, but also to other countries – namely Iran – who are also increasingly going down the same route taken by North Korea.

In addition, the US has used sanctions to pursue a range of its own grand-strategic objectives in the context of its relationships with its great-power counterparts. Washington's cooperation with and support for Japan's sanctions resolutions at the UNSC, for example, can be seen as advancing a relatively longstanding American strategy of trying to encourage Tokyo to embrace a greater leadership role, both regionally and at the global level. Supporting this interpretation, two eminent American commentators, Richard L. Armitage and Joseph S. Nye, have recently observed:

> Japan's new leaders are arguing for a more proactive security and diplomatic role that will keep Japan's weight in the international system high. The United States needs a Japan that is confident and engaged in that way ... Not to encourage Japan to play a more active role in support of international stability and security is to deny the international community Japan's full potential.[24]

The American use of sanctions in the context of the North Korea nuclear crisis can also be viewed as part of a larger effort to shape the course of the Sino-US strategic relationship. Securing some degree of Chinese cooperation with American sanctioning strategies is one technique which US policymakers have employed in an effort to 'encourage Beijing to seek increased influence through diplomatic and economic interactions ... and to use that influence in a manner that improves the prospects for security and economic prosperity in Asia and around the world.'[25] Simultaneously, and yet seemingly in direct contradiction of this interpretation, the US's efforts to secure Chinese cooperation with its sanctioning strategies can also been seen as part of an effort to create a degree of distance in the historically intimate China–North Korea strategic relationship. Beijing's support for UN sanctions and its cooperation with Washington in the Banco Delta Asia episode have occasioned some cooling in relations between Beijing and Pyongyang. The opening of a rift between them is significant from China's perspective for reasons that go well beyond the North Korean nuclear crisis, and which relate directly to the issue of Taiwan. This, in turn, goes some way towards explaining Washington's continuing efforts to ensure Chinese support for UN sanctions, even though it often has to agree to more diluted measures than US policymakers would ideally prefer.

Japanese sanctions

Within a relatively short space of time, Japan has gone from being a reluctant employer of sanctions against North Korea to one of – if not the – most frequent users of those instruments against that country. During the 1993–94 North Korean nuclear crisis, for instance, Japan came under heavy pressure to join US-led sanctions against the North – which it largely managed to avert because of the Clinton administration's shift to a policy of engagement with Pyongyang.[26] Even as recently as March 2003, Tokyo once again resisted US pressure to apply sanctions against the North, arguing instead that the crisis should be resolved through a multilateral forum and that Washington and Pyongyang could usefully conduct bilateral negotiations on the sidelines of that forum.[27] The one clear exception to Tokyo's traditional opposition to the use of sanctions against North Korea came following Pyongyang's August 1998 test of a *Taepo-dong* ballistic missile, which passed over the Northern part of the main Japanese island of Honshu. Japan responded to this development by suspending its funding for the Korean Peninsula Energy Development Organisation (KEDO) – the body charged with overseeing implementation of the 1994 Agreed Framework – and food aid to North Korea, as well as charter flights and normalisation talks between the two countries.[28] By and large, however, prior to 2003 Tokyo's default position on the use of sanctions against North Korea was that such measures should only be applied in the event they were authorised by a UN resolution or as the result of a multinational agreement. Indeed, this was a legal requirement under the terms of Japan's Foreign Exchange and Foreign Trade Control Law.

In May 2003, Prime Minister Junichiro Koizumi announced in the lead-up to a meeting with President Bush that Japan could apply sanctions involving the blocking of Japanese remittances to North Korea, which the US had been requesting. Koizumi's reinterpretation of the Foreign Exchange and Foreign Trade Control Law resulted from a debate within his government over how many countries were required to constitute an 'international effort' as far as the employment of sanctions was concerned. This requirement of the legislation was reinterpreted to mean two countries, of which Japan would obviously be one and, in this instance, the US the second.[29] In late January 2004, the Lower House of the Japanese Diet went even further by amending the Foreign Exchange and Foreign Trade Control Law to allow Japan to unilaterally cut off remittances and to also enforce an import ban against North Korea which, while not the explicit target of the measure, was clearly foremost in the minds of those voting in favour of the amendment. The Upper House went on in February 2004 to pass this amendment to the legislation; and during the following month, it also introduced a second piece of legislation calling upon Japan to ban all port calls from North Korean vessels.[30]

The amendment marked the beginning of a period during which the Japanese use of unilateral sanctions against North Korea was to intensify. In March 2005, for instance, a further piece of legislation dealing with liability for oil pollution was amended to require all foreign vessels weighing more than 100 tonnes to be insured in order to be able to enter Japanese ports. As only 2.5% of the estimated 1,000 North Korean vessels which docked at Japanese ports actually had such insurance, this measure essentially amounted to a de facto sanction against the North.[31] Japan imposed further unilateral sanctions against North Korea following its July 2006 missile tests, which included barring a North Korean ferry accused of complicity in Pyongyang's illegal activities – the *Mangyongbong-92* – from making port calls in Japan, as well as banning North Korean officials from entering Japan.[32] These sanctions were strengthened significantly following North Korea's October 2006 nuclear test, after which Tokyo barred all North Korean ships from Japanese ports, introduced a ban on all North Korean imports and prohibited North Korean nationals from entering Japan.[33] A similar pattern was repeated in the aftermath of the North Korean rocket launch and nuclear test of 2009. In April of that year, Tokyo responded to the North Korean rocket launch by reducing the level of Japanese remittances permitted to North Korea from 30m to 10m yen, while also reducing the amount of Japanese currency permitted in North Korea from 1m to 300,000 yen.[34] Following the North Korean nuclear test of May 2009, Tokyo implemented a complete ban on all Japanese trade with the North.[35]

Japan has implemented a range of other sanctions against North Korean interests during the period in question. Measures have been applied against the General Association of Korean residents in Japan (or Chongryun), which for much of the history of Japan–North Korea relations has enjoyed de facto diplomatic status. In February 2006, however, some of the preferential tax treatment which the Chongryun had previously enjoyed was revoked, while in the following month Japanese Police conducted – their first ever raids on six Chongryun offices.[36] Restrictions have also been placed on Japan's *Pachinko* parlours, many of which are owned by ethnic Koreans with sympathies towards the North, hence providing a significant source of revenue for Pyongyang. Japanese businesses have been generally supportive of Tokyo's efforts to apply sanctions against North Korea. In her recent study of Japan's 'economic diplomacy' towards North Korea, for instance, Asian studies researcher Maaike Okano-Heijmans quotes from an interview with a prominent Japanese businessman who said:

> It is unacceptable barbaric behaviour that North Korea performed a nuclear test, disregarding the restraints of the United Nations and the entire world. It is only natural that the UN and Japan deal with this in a stricter manner, and we as private businesses will adopt an attitude along the government's line.[37]

Consistent with these remarks and also with its traditional preference for sanctions applied in multilateral settings, Japan has been highly supportive and proactive in terms of developing and implementing UN measures. Following the July 2006 North Korean missile tests, for instance, Japan wasted little time in requesting that the Security Council call an urgent meeting and provided a draft sanctions resolution. Likewise, in the wake of the October 2006 North Korean nuclear test Tokyo cooperated closely with Washington to push for the implementation of UNSCR 1718. Japan has also worked assiduously to implement the various Security Council resolutions. In November 2006, for example, it implemented Resolution 1718 and banned the export of 24 luxury goods from Japan to North Korea. Beyond the UN, Japan has also been a prominent member of the Proliferation Security Initiative, hosting maritime inter diction exercises in October 2004 and October 2007.

Japanese motivations for applying sanctions against North Korea are threefold. First and foremost, sanctions have been employed for domestic reasons related to the as yet unresolved issue of Japanese citizens abducted by North Korea during the 1970s and 1980s. From Tokyo's perspective, the main points of contention here concern the number of Japanese citizens kidnapped by the North and their fate. The issue remains a heated one in Japanese domestic politics and receives widespread coverage in the Japanese media. Protests by the families of the abductees are frequent, such as that held in June 2005 when approximately 100 families and their supporters gathered outside Prime Minister Koizumi's offices. Responding to such pressure, successive Japanese governments have refused to provide North Korea with foreign aid or to normalise diplomatic relations between the two countries until the issue is resolved.

Secondly, Tokyo has also used sanctions with a view to influencing Pyongyang's policies, particularly in relation to the abductions issue and the North Korean nuclear crisis. Regarding the first of these issues, in November 2003 Koizumi famously threatened to apply sanctions against North Korea in the event Pyongyang continued to refuse to address the abductions issue. Like the US, Japan has also employed the relaxation of sanctions as an instrument of statecraft in relation to this issue, agreeing in June 2008 to partially lift sanctions against North Korea after Pyongyang pledged to open a new investigation into the abductions.[38] With little progress made on this issue and in response to domestic pressure, however, in October 2008 Tokyo announced that it would ultimately not be lifting the sanctions in question.[39] As for the North Korean nuclear issue, in May 2005 Shinzo Abe – then a senior official in the Liberal Democratic Party (LDP) of Japan – indicated that sanctions would likely be applied against the North should the diplomatic route provided by the Six-Party Talks fail to deliver a solution to the nuclear crisis.[40] Consistent with this, the Japanese Cabinet in March 2007 approved the extension of sanctions imposed against North Korea following its October 2006 nuclear test in an attempt to pressure Pyongyang into shutting down its Yongbyon nuclear reactor, as it had pledged to do under the terms of a February 2007 agreement coming out of the Six-Party Talks.[41]

Finally, Tokyo has also employed sanctions in the context of the North Korean nuclear crisis with a view to demonstrating its capacity for leadership in regional and global affairs. Despite the fact that it has become increasingly engaged in a range of peacekeeping operations (such as those in Cambodia, East Timor, Mozambique and the Golan Heights), disaster-relief operations (such as that following the 2004 Indian Ocean tsunami) and as a member of 'coalitions of the willing' (deploying, for instance, to the Indian Ocean and Iraq in the context of the 'war on terror'), Japan remains a country that, in the words of the eminent scholar of Japanese security Richard Samuels, 'may still be punching below its weight in world affairs'.[42] This is partly a reflection of the fact that Japan remains bound by its own constitutional constraints. Sanctions in this context provide an obvious coercive alternative to the threat or use of force, allowing Japan the option of demonstrating leadership, as it did following the July 2006 North Korean missile tests. Tokyo's activism was pivotal in pushing through UNSCR 1718. In this case as well as through the initiation of UNSCR 1874 – which was advanced by Japan, the US and South Korea – Tokyo has used sanctions to demonstrate its value as an American ally.

Chinese sanctions

China too has gone from being a reluctant user of sanctions against North Korea to a more frequent invoker – albeit far more reluctant than Japan. As recently as March 2003, for example, a Chinese official publicly expressed the view that 'sanctions aren't an appropriate method and will only complicate the [North Korean] situation.'[43] Consistent with this, Chinese officials during the same month refused to participate in meetings to draft a UNSC statement condemning North Korea's nuclear activities, largely on the grounds that the next logical step following the issuing of such a statement would have been the imposition of sanctions against Pyongyang.[44] The logic underpinning China's official position on the use of sanctions vis-à-vis North Korea was essentially twofold: Beijing maintained that China's trading relations with North Korea were completely separate from the nuclear issue and that the former should not therefore be interrupted in the interests of seeking a resolution to the latter.[45] It was of the view that less coercive approaches should be given more time to work before sanctions could even be contemplated because, it argued, the prospects for these influencing Pyongyang's policies were more favourable.[46]

Beijing's traditional opposition to the use of sanctions is founded largely on the premise that these instruments violate a core Chinese foreign-policy principle of non-interference. In the case of North Korea, additional security, historical and strategic considerations have been significant in Chinese thinking. In security terms, Chinese policymakers were concerned about

the unpredictability of Pyongyang's response to the imposition
of sanctions; they fear the North might respond militarily to any
such development based upon its previous statements during
the 1993–94 nuclear crisis (that it would turn Seoul into a 'sea
of fire'). A military response of the part of Pyongyang would,
from China's perspective, have had a destabilising regional
impact, which would threaten China's impressive economic
growth rates.

Beijing was also concerned regarding the potential for
sanctions to generate serious economic dislocation in the
North, creating an implosion of the regime and, subsequently,
sending a flood of refugees across China's border with North
Korea. From a historical perspective, China was also reluctant
to impose sanctions against the North given the traditional
defence ties between the two nations. China suffered – according to one official Chinese estimate – approximately 360,000
combat losses and more than 380,000 non-combat losses during
the Korean War, creating a strong historical bond between the
two countries.[47] In strategic terms, Beijing also viewed the
maintenance of close relations with Pyongyang in the context
of its emerging strategic competition with the US, particularly
given the capacity of the North Korean armed forces to act as
a counter to America's military assets in South Korea. As arms
control expert Professor Shen Dingli observes:

> Even though the likelihood of China and the United
> States going to war with each other ... is increas-
> ingly low, both sides cannot rule out that possibility
> completely. As a result, both sides are preparing strat-
> egies for the worst-case scenario, while strategists
> in Pyongyang are trying to figure out ways to take
> advantage of this mutual hedging between China and
> the United States to further their own interests.[48]

US policymakers have consistently urged Beijing to use its close relationship with the North to influence Pyongyang's nuclear policies. Particular emphasis has been given to North Korea's growing level of economic dependence upon China as a potential source of leverage here. Although the data remain extraordinarily murky, most reliable estimates suggest that China provides North Korea with approximately 90% of its oil, 80% of its consumer goods and 45% of its food. Indicative of the substantial and, indeed, rising gap in two-way trade between the two countries, North Korea currently has a $994.6m trade deficit with China.[49] With this in mind, in April 2005 US Assistant Secretary of State Christopher Hill reiterated a proposal – first put forward in 2003 by US National Security Advisor Condoleezza Rice – that China could execute a 'technical' interruption of North Korea's fuel supplies as a means of exerting leverage against Pyongyang. To the chagrin of the Americans, Beijing responded to this proposal by asserting that such a step was simply not possible on the grounds that the high paraffin content of the crude oil would result in a clogging of the pipelines and necessitate their replacement.[50]

Interestingly, however, from 2003 onwards Beijing has shown an increased willingness to apply a range of unilateral sanctions against North Korea. In March of that year, for example, China is thought to have cut off an oil pipeline to North Korea for a period of three days. Although Beijing claims that this development was not intentional and was, instead, the result of 'technical difficulties', speculation exists that it was actually a move designed to pressure Pyongyang into participating in three-way talks with China and the US. According to one line of thinking, Beijing was seeking to send a message to North Korea that more sustained sanctions could follow if it opted not to participate in these proliferation talks – a rationale refuted, according to some analysts, by the fact that Beijing has typically used incentives rather than sanctions in seeking North Korean participation in dialogues addressing the nuclear problem. During the period since, however, China has reportedly periodically reduced its oil supplies to the North – between September and November 2006 and again in February and March 2007 – apparently with a view to influencing Pyongyang's nuclear policies. China assisted US efforts to impose financial sanctions by freezing North Korean bank accounts at Banco Delta Asia – admittedly for reasons that also related to protecting the reputation of Chinese banks – and imposed further financial sanctions following the North Korean nuclear test of October 2006. Chinese military sales to North Korea have also been substantially restricted over the past half decade, with North Korea now acquiring the bulk of its military hardware from Russia and Kazakhstan.[51] Chinese officials have even reportedly contemplated imposing food sanctions against the North on the grounds that such measures 'would have the greatest impact on Pyongyang'.[52] Ultimately, however, such measures have thus far been avoided for humanitarian reasons and out of concern for the social instability that these sanctions might precipitate in North Korea.

Although China traditionally followed a strategy of 'abstention' or 'non-participation' when voting at the Security Council,[53] over recent years it has committed to all three resolutions targeting North Korea. This is despite the fact that each has contained increasingly tougher sanctions measures. In the case of UNSCR 1695, for example, China eventually agreed to sign on to the draft resolution provided by Japan – after tabling a much milder draft version of its own – but only once explicit references to Chapter VII of the UN Charter, which would have permitted the use of military force in response to North Korean provocations, were dropped.[54] Chinese support for Resolution 1718 was even more forthcoming. In the words of one respected analyst, the resolution 'was unprecedented in the speed of its reaction and in the lengths to which China was willing to go to punish North Korea'.[55] However, Beijing once again insisted that explicit references to Chapter VII of the UN Charter be excluded and that implementation of the sanctions be left to individual states. It was less inclined to support the application of sanctions through the UN following North Korea's April 2009 rocket launch, supporting Pyongyang's right to launch a satellite and to the 'peaceful' use of outer space. On this occasion, Beijing strongly opposed the introduction of a new resolution, favouring instead the issuing of a UNSC Presidential Statement renewing sanctions imposed under Resolution 1718. Following North Korea's May 2009 nuclear test, China exhibited greater willingness to support a Security Council Resolution. Once again, however, it continued to insist that priority be given to a diplomatic solution to the North Korea nuclear crisis and that implementation of resolution 1874 be left in the hands of individual member countries.

This lingering reluctance to use the full force of sanctions aside, what is clear is that China's comfort levels with employing these instruments has unquestionably risen since 2003. This trend is reflected in surveys conducted by *Global Times*, an English-language newspaper published by the Chinese Communist Party. One recent poll, for example, revealed that approximately two-thirds of the Chinese public felt that Beijing should be taking even stronger actions, including the use of sanctions, to resolve the North Korean nuclear problem. Similarly, half of the 20 leading Chinese foreign-policy experts polled by the newspaper expressed their support for the use of tougher sanctions measures against Pyongyang.[56] A number of factors explain this growing willingness to employ sanctions in the context of the North Korean nuclear crisis. Beijing views its support for UNSC sanctions against North Korea, in particular, as part of a larger strategy of projecting an image of 'responsible' great powerhood and, concurrently, of building a more robust and constructive bilateral relationship with the US.[57] Secondly, it reflects Beijing's growing frustration with the Kim Jong-il regime, insofar as Pyongyang's provocations have undermined Beijing's efforts to deliver a diplomatic solution to the North Korean crisis through the Six-Party Talks process. China's recent support for UNSCR 1874, for example, was partly a reflection of its desire to punish Pyongyang, which reportedly provided the Chinese leadership with less than 30 minutes' warning that the May 2009 nuclear test was about to take place.[58]

The defining characteristic of China's use of sanctions against North Korea, however, has been the discrete manner in which it has employed these instruments. Indeed, albeit somewhat counter-intuitively, a strong case can be made that the greater the level of discretion exercised by China in applying sanctions against North Korea, the more serious its intention to genuinely influence Pyongyang's policies and behaviour. This can be seen with reference to the range of unilateral sanctions that China reportedly has levelled against Pyongyang, which have typically been applied in a quite secretive manner but clearly also with a view to influencing the calculus of the Kim Jong-il regime. This suggests that China does see sanctions as an instrument with the potential to perform certain instrumental functions, such as encouraging North Korea to return to the negotiating table during periods when the Six-Party Talks have stalled. It ought to be noted, of course, that the application of these measures has not been cost-free for China, often leading to a subsequent cooling in relations with Pyongyang.[59] Yet Beijing still appears to feel far more comfortable with the unilateral, as opposed to the multilateral, application of sanctions, largely due to the greater ability that it has to control the manner in which these measures are implemented.[60] Consistent with this, although China's willingness to support multilateral measures via the UNSC route has certainly increased over the course of the North Korean nuclear crisis, its support has remained somewhat circumspect and Beijing has remained relatively steadfast in seeking to protect Pyongyang from the potentially most crippling sanctions measures.

Russian and EU sanctions

Relative to the other great powers examined in this chapter, the influence and involvement of both the EU and Russia has been negligible in the context of the North Korean nuclear crisis examined here. This was not always the case. Indeed, during the early years of the twenty-first century there existed a degree of optimism that either of these two actors might potentially be able to help broker a solution to the crisis. During this period the EU took a keen interest in North Korean nuclear matters, as reflected by its membership – along with the US, Japan and South Korea – on the Executive Board of KEDO. Brussels established diplomatic relations with Pyongyang in May 2001, at which time it strongly favoured a strategy of engagement. Indeed, as recently as 2003 the EU was publicly opposing the use of sanctions against North Korea. On the eve of a visit to Seoul in February of that year, for instance, EU foreign policy chief Javier Solana stated: 'I don't think it is the moment to impose sanctions. I think sanctions will contribute to the opposite of what we want to take – which is to defuse the crisis.'[61]

Hopes were also high during the early part of the twenty-first century that Moscow too might be able to deliver a solution to the protracted North Korean nuclear crisis. Indeed, according to one analyst writing in early 2003, a time at which diplomatic negotiations had stalled following Assistant Secretary of State James Kelly's October 2002 allegations of a secret uranium-enrichment programme: 'Russia may be best positioned to open negotiations with North Korea.'[62] This hope stemmed partly from the fact that North Korea and the former Soviet Union enjoyed close ties during the Cold War given their shared communist ideology. Interestingly, however, Moscow's influence had diminished considerably during the 1990s, particularly as Pyongyang opted to deal directly with the Clinton administration. Russia re-inserted itself into the diplomacy surrounding the North Korean crisis in July 2000, however, when President Vladimir Putin undertook a historic visit to Pyongyang – a visit which was reciprocated by the North Korean leader Kim Jong-il. Immediately following North Korea's withdrawal from the Nuclear Non-Proliferation Treaty (NPT) in early January 2003, Russia again sought to sought to seize the diplomatic initiative by proposing a 'package plan' which included a security guarantee for North Korea, humanitarian and economic assistance, as well as the establishment of a nuclear-free zone on the Korean Peninsula.[63] During this period, Russian officials repeatedly voiced their opposition to the use of sanctions, such as in late January 2003 when Foreign Minister Igor Ivanov asserted: 'Today it would be unjustifiable to resort to any methods of pressure on North Korea via sanctions or via threats, because this might make the situation even more difficult.'[64]

Brussels has become more accepting of the application of sanctions both generally and specifically, in the case of North Korea – largely in reaction to the first North Korean nuclear test of October 2006. To date, the EU has implemented all three UNSC resolutions containing sanctions against Kim Jong-il's regime. It has also exhibited some willingness to go further by adding sanctions of its own. When implementing UNSCR1718 in November 2006, for instance, the Council of the European Union extended this resolution 'to cover other conventional weapons, including at least all goods and technology on the EU Common List of Military Equipment'.[65] Similarly, in July 2009 it adopted a reinforced version of Resolution 1874 that included the 'autonomous listing of items subject to export ban, autonomous listing of person and entities subject to travel ban and asset freeze, enhanced financial vigilance and reinforced cargo inspections'.[66] Reflecting the EU's growing comfort with the use of sanctions against North Korea, the vice-president of the European Commission, Guenter Verheugen, in July 2006 expressed EU support for the strongly worded draft resolution tabled by Japan following the North Korean missile tests and argued in favour of robust sanctions by expressing the view that 'it is better to have no resolution than a bad resolution.'[67] However, according to a prominent European commentator on North Korean matters, Axel Berkofsky, it is also an indication of a growing EU frustration at being a 'payer' as opposed to a 'player' in the diplomatic manoeuvrings surrounding the North Korean crisis.[68]

Russia, in contrast, has exhibited far greater reticence than the EU on the issue of applying sanctions against North Korea. When implementing UNSCR 1718, for example, Moscow defined 'luxury goods' so narrowly – to include items such as fur coats costing more than $9,637 and watches costing $2,000 – as to make the application of those measures virtually meaningless.[69] Moscow also joined Beijing following the July 2006 North Korean missiles tests by initially opposing the strong draft resolution tabled by Japan. Admittedly, Moscow did facilitate (at Washington's request) the lifting of the Banco Delta Asia sanctions against North Korea when, in June 2007, it negotiated the release of $24m in North Korean accounts to the Russian Central bank.[70] Like China, however, following the April 2009 North Korean rocket launch Russia subsequently opposed the introduction of any new resolution on the basis of Pyongyang's claims that the rocket was used to launch a satellite.[71]

The Russian stance has nevertheless hardened somewhat in recent years, despite its continuing desire to protect Pyongyang and to avoid taking action that might provoke Kim Jong-il. UNSC Resolution 1874, in response to the May 2009 North Korean nuclear test, met with 'unprecedented' support from Moscow, which insisted only that the searching of suspect shipping should not be mandatory for all states. A number of factors explain this subtle shift in approach. Firstly, Russia has become increasingly concerned regarding the prospect of a North Korean missile test going astray and sending debris on to its territory. Indeed, like Japan, Moscow has publicly discussed the possibility of using surface-to-air missiles to protect its territory from the possibility of 'failed' North Korean test launches.[72] Russia is also apprehensive about North Korea's burgeoning nuclear and missile capabilities and, particularly, the ramifications of these for broader regional stability.[73] Secondly and perhaps most importantly, however, with China becoming increasingly open to the initiation of sanctions against North Korea, Moscow has felt a degree of pressure to follow or risk being exposed as the only great power unwilling to support – ostensibly at least – international efforts to oppose Pyongyang's provocations.

Assessment and analysis

As was the case during the 1993–94 North Korea nuclear crisis, Pyongyang has continued to react aggressively to the threat or use of sanctions against it. Using language reminiscent of that employed by Pyongyang during that earlier crisis, the Kim Jong-il regime in January 2003 responded to suggestions that sanctions could be employed against it through the UN Security Council by asserting that such action would be regarded as 'tantamount to war.'[74] Perhaps the North's most bellicose repudiation of threatened sanctions came several months later in June 2003, when it threatened 'limitless retaliation' against the imposition of US-led sanctions. Interestingly, Pyongyang suggested that Japan, rather than South Korea, would be the target on this occasion.[75] Similar language has been employed throughout the course of the more recent North Korean nuclear crisis that provides the focus for this chapter. As recently as June 2009, for instance, Pyongyang responded to the introduction of UNSCR 1874 by pledging to continue to advance its nuclear programme and to take 'firm military action if the United States and its allies try to isolate us'.[76]

These consistently hostile reactions notwithstanding, there is little if any evidence to suggest that the application of sanctions against North Korea has had any meaningful effect on Pyongyang's decision-making calculus. Those concessions which North Korea has made – and it is difficult to discern whether these have been made as a consequence of sanctions or the Six-Party Talks diplomatic process (or, indeed, due to the combined influence of sanctions and diplomacy) – have tended to be superficial and temporary at best. In June 2008, for instance, North Korea handed over some 18,000 pages of documentation from its Yongbyon nuclear facilities. Ironically, these were subsequently discovered to carry traces of enriched uranium.[77] Pyongyang also provided a declaration of its plutonium holdings and blew up a cooling tower at the Yongbyon facility. Yet, as Mark Fitzpatrick observes, within only a year of these developments, the North completed fresh tests of its most destructive weapons, resumed plutonium reprocessing, unveiled a uranium-enrichment programme, annulled the Korean War armistice, declared void all bilateral agreements with South Korea and all multilateral agreements from the Six-Party Talks, and threatened 'merciless nuclear attacks if nations implement[ed] measures adopted by the Security Council in response to North Korea's provocations'.[78]

The apparent inability of sanctions to alter Pyongyang's nuclear policies is not entirely unsurprising. North Korea, after all, remains a destitute country facing chronic economic, energy and humanitarian problems. Its nuclear programme and, to a lesser extent, its ballistic-missile programme, essentially constitute the only remaining bargaining chips with which the Kim Jong-il regime can barter with the outside world. Moreover, all indications are that the North Korean leadership harbours an acute sense of insecurity and fear of external invasion by the US – a fear which was noticeably heightened by the March 2003 invasion of Iraq. Against that backdrop, a strong case can be made that Pyongyang's reluctance to alter its nuclear policies is largely to be expected – even in the face of increasingly harsher sanctions.

This is not to suggest that sanctions imposed against North Korea have had no impact whatsoever in terms of the costs they have imposed on Pyongyang. Sanctions targeting Banco Delta Asia appear to have carried significant implications for the North's economy, and caused the greatest concern to the Kim Jong-il regime. This was primarily because these measures made other international lending institutions reluctant to provide hard currency – namely in US dollars, euros and Japanese yen – which Pyongyang requires for legal and illegal trade. As Gottemoeller observes: 'In short order banks and financial institutions around the world were unwilling to handle the funds of the North Korean regime, concerned about attracting one of the new "special measures" enacted under the Patriot Act.'[79] Similarly, during the early twenty-first century, Japanese financial sanctions caused remittances from North Korean sympathisers to plummet from more than $100m a year to approximately a quarter of that level.[80]

It is also widely assumed that the imposition of sanctions has impacted psychologically upon the leadership in Pyongyang, particularly given the creeping willingness of Beijing and Moscow to sign up to these measures. During the Cold War, North Korea enjoyed the backing of two major-power patrons, the Soviet Union and China. Each provided it with substantial economic and military support. The strategic value of the latter was particularly evident during the Korean War of 1950–53, when Chinese intervention rescued the North from military defeat. Since the end of the Cold War, however, Chinese and Russian ties with the North have weakened. While both continue to demonstrate some proclivity towards protecting Pyongyang from the worst effects of sanctions, their willingness to sign up to UNSC measures – most recently in the 'unprecedented' level of support each exhibited in signing up to Resolution 1874 – would appear to have had the effect of increasing North Korea's sense of isolation.

One of the other rare points of commonality between US and Chinese policymakers regarding the use of sanctions against North Korea has been a desire to employ these instruments with a view to bringing Pyongyang to the negotiating table and to accept steps towards denuclearisation. However, it is difficult to determine the impact of sanctions in terms of achieving particular objectives. The US intelligence community, for instance, often refers to North Korea as the 'blackest of black holes' given the difficulties of obtaining information relating to this extremely closed society and its paranoid leadership. By way of example, one piece of evidence frequently cited to support the hypothesis that sanctions have been successful in encouraging Pyongyang to negotiate is Kim Jong-il's November 2006 agreement to return to the Six-Party Talks. This took place only a matter of weeks after the Security Council introduced Resolution 1718, and brought the parties back to the table after a hiatus of approximately one year.[81] In reality, it is virtually impossible to discern with any degree of certainty whether sanctions prompted this decision, or whether Pyongyang's apparent policy shift was nothing more than a clever ruse designed to dilute the unusually high level of international support for those measures. Some commentators have even gone so far as to suggest that Pyongyang was actually using the issue of sanctions as a stalling tactic to buy more time to advance its nuclear-weapons programme. Since North Korean negotiators were reportedly authorised only to discuss US financial sanctions during Six-Party Talks in December 2006, this suspicion could be well founded.[82]

Above all else, however, the ability of sanctions to influence Pyongyang's nuclear policies has been seriously undermined due to the fact that the most enthusiastic employer of these instruments, the US, conducts virtually no trade with North Korea. Similarly, Japan – which was the North's second largest trading partner less than a decade ago –has been overtaken by South Korea, India, Russia and Thailand, in large part as a direct consequence of the trade restrictions it has levied against Pyongyang. [83] China, of course, remains North Korea's number one trading partner and has increased its economic interaction significantly in the past decade.[84] Two of the North's closest trading partners, China and Russia, have worked to dilute the nature and scope of international sanctions against it, thereby protecting Pyongyang from the potentially most crippling of these measures.

Interestingly, despite the apparently limited capacity of sanctions to influence Pyongyang's behaviour, each of the great powers considered in this chapter has found benefits to employing these instruments which go beyond those traditionally emphasised by sanctions scholars. Consistent with what sanctions scholars have long recognised, of course, the US has employed sanctions to send 'signals' to third parties – such as Iran – that a similar fate awaits them should they continue on a similar nuclear path as North Korea.[85] Beyond that objective and in line with this study's central argument, however, American policymakers have found sanctions useful in terms of encouraging Japan to play a greater leadership role in developing UNSC resolutions. Somewhat paradoxically, the US has also employed sanctions to encourage Beijing to seek increased global and regional influence and, concurrently, to put strategically significant distance between China and North Korea. China has also signed on to US-led sanctions introduced through the UN with a view to deepening Sino-American cooperation and in order to project an image of great-power responsibility. The European Union has increasingly invoked sanctions during the North Korean nuclear crisis with the intention of becoming more instrumental in the diplomacy surrounding this crisis. Finally, in perhaps the most apt illustration of how sanctions can be used as an instrument to influence and shape strategic relationships between the great powers, Russia has come under increasing pressure to support sanctions imposed through the Security Council lest it be exposed as the only great power unwilling to support international efforts to oppose Pyongyang's provocations.

CHAPTER THREE

Sanctioning Iran

The Iranian nuclear crisis has entered a period of renewed tension over recent months. A clandestine enrichment facility was exposed in September 2009, near the northern city of Qom. Responding to international criticism of its secrecy in building the plant, Tehran in November 2009 defiantly announced its intention to build a further ten enrichment plants. The crisis further deepened in January 2010, when Iran missed a 31 December 2009 deadline for accepting a deal, proposed through the International Atomic Energy Agency (IAEA), to send approximately three-quarters of its low-enriched uranium stockpile offshore to Russia for further enrichment for subsequent fabrication into fuel rods (for the Tehran research reactor) in France. In February 2010, the colourful and controversial Iranian president Mahmoud Ahmadinejad subsequently declared Iran a 'nuclear power' and announced Tehran's intention to raise the enrichment level of its uranium from a maximum of 3.5% to the 20% level needed for the research-reactor fuel, thus bringing it a step closer to the estimated 90% mark required for a nuclear weapon. Shortly after enrichment to the 20% level commenced, the IAEA issued a report which, for the first time in this crisis, expressed concerns that Iran's 'past or current undisclosed activities related to the development of a nuclear payload for a missile'.[1]

A chorus of calls for further sanctions against Iran have erupted in the wake of these developments. The US Treasury Department imposed new targeted financial measures against four companies and an Iranian national for their alleged complicity in Iran's nuclear activities. US President Barack Obama projected the establishment of a new 'significant regime of sanctions that will indicate to [Iran] how isolated they are from the international community as a whole'.[2] The European Union has threatened 'very strong sanctions' in response to Iran's self-proclaimed 'nuclear power' status.[3] Israeli Prime Minister Benjamin Netanyahu has gone even further, calling for 'crippling sanctions' to be imposed against Iran, insisting that such measures 'must be applied right now'.[4]

However, the chances that sanctions may end up altering Tehran's decision-making calculus or ultimately providing a silver bullet to the Iranian nuclear crisis do not look particularly promising at the time of writing. Tehran has reacted defiantly in the face of such calls, asserting it 'will never give up enrichment at any price. Even the threat of military attack will not stop us.'[5] China, a central player in this crisis, has been particularly vocal in its opposition to the prospect of additional sanctions being applied against Iran. Given Beijing's veto power on the Security Council, the prospects for introducing sanctions with genuine 'bite' via this route do not thus appear promising.[6] Moreover, given the delicate current state of Iran's domestic political situation, even the Obama administration is showing signs of backing away from the most potent measures on offer – those limiting Iran's ability to import gasoline and other refined products – for fear of undermining anti-government forces by encouraging the

Iranian populace to rally behind the incumbent regime in the face of external international pressure.[7] If further sanctions appear such a shaky proposition even before they have been conceived and introduced, what then explains mounting international pressure for their imposition?

Background

Iranian interest in developing a nuclear-weapons capability dates back to the Iran–Iraq War (1980–88). Iran commenced a uranium-enrichment programme in response to chemical weapons attacks.[8] The programme was to remain secret for almost two decades, even though suspicions began to mount during the 1990s that Iran was moving down the nuclear path. Yet it was not until an exiled Iranian dissident group dramatically announced the existence of two secret nuclear facilities during an August 2002 press conference in Washington DC that the world came to know about the Iranian nuclear programme. An IAEA inspection went on to confirm the existence of these two facilities – a uranium-enrichment plant at Natanz, in central Iran, and a heavy water plant in Arak, in the north of the country. This essentially marked the beginning of the Iranian nuclear crisis.

The international community responded to these developments with widespread condemnation, while at the same time serious efforts were made to engage with Iran, which insisted its nuclear activities were for peaceful purposes, primarily related to the provision of energy. These claims persist, despite rich oil and gas resources that make the development of nuclear power uneconomical – and despite the fact that Tehran kept its nuclear facilities hidden from the world. Nevertheless, with the 'E-3' of the UK, France and Germany taking the lead, a series of negotiations continued until 2005. At the heart of these was the European demand for cessation of enrichment-related activity; Iran repeatedly declared its intent to keep its enrichment programme.

In October 2003 Iran agreed to temporarily suspend enrichment in exchange for not having its case referred to the Security Council, where it feared the sanctions that might be applied. Yet serious disagreement quickly emerged as to precisely what the suspension was supposed to cover, and by early 2004 it was becoming increasingly apparent that Iran was exploiting the ambiguity to essentially violate the spirit of it. In April of that year Iran informed the IAEA of its intention to conduct 'hot tests' at its uranium-conversion facility at Esfahan and subsequently went on to convert a small amount of natural uranium into uranium hexafluoride (or UF_6, the feed material used for enrichment). In July 2004 Iran then forced the IAEA to remove the seals on its nuclear equipment and resumed uranium enrichment-related activities. At this point, the US – which had been calling for sanctions from June 2003 when safeguards violations were first documented by IAEA inspectors – reiterated calls for the imposition of sanctions through the UNSC. While members of the IAEA Board of Governors gave initial indications that they would support such a course and refer the matter upwards, the Board backed away from that threat in November 2004 after Iran again agreed to temporarily and voluntarily suspend its uranium-enrichment activities in the context of ongoing negotiations with the E-3.

Any sense of renewed optimism that the Iranian nuclear conundrum could be resolved through diplomatic channels was short-lived, however, and the crisis came to a head in 2005 when the agreement with the E-3 broke down. The probability that Iran's programme was linked to a nuclear weapons programme was further reinforced in March 2005 when the Pakistani government confirmed Iranian involvement in the A.Q. Khan international arms-smuggling network. In the lead-up to the June 2005 presidential election – which would subsequently see Ahmadinejad come to power – the Iranian leadership, with Supreme Leader Ayatollah Khamenei at its helm, became increasingly resolute in expressing the view that Iran would not relinquish its uranium-enrichment capabilities. Indeed, in the weeks immediately prior to the election of Ahmadinejad, departing President Mohammad Khatami indicated that Iran would resume uranium conversion (a precursor to enrichment), regardless of what incentives were put before it by the Europeans. This step was subsequently taken on 8 August 2005, six days after Khatami stepped down.

In the wake of these developments, the IAEA Board of Governors in September 2005 found Iran to be in non-compliance, but it did not report the issue to the UN Security Council until February 2006, after Iran resumed uranium enrichment. Iran responded by further curtailing cooperation with the IAEA, and after a period of negotiation the UNSC on 31 July 2006 passed Resolution 1696, which called for Iran to suspend its uranium-enrichment activities within a month and fully cooperate with the IAEA or face the possibility of economic and diplomatic sanctions.[9] That deadline ultimately passed without Iran taking any corrective action.

Acting under Article 41 of chapter VII of the UN Charter, the Security Council responded to Iran's non-compliance by adopting Resolution 1737 on 23 December 2006. This was the first in a series of three UNSC resolutions containing sanctions pertaining specifically to Iran. UNSCR 1737 required Iran to immediately suspend all enrichment-related and reprocessing activities, as well as work on all heavy water-related projects. It placed restrictions upon IAEA technical assistance projects with Iran, which the agency's Board of Governors subsequently implemented in one of its rare sanctions moves. Resolution 1737 also called upon all member states to implement a number of sanctions measures targeting Iran's nuclear and ballistic missile programmes. Firstly, it required steps to be taken to prevent the supply of materials and technology which could further Iran's enrichment-related, reprocessing and heavy water-related activities, or that could assist with the advancement of its nuclear-weapon delivery systems. Secondly, Resolution 1737 called upon all states to avoid providing Iran with technical or financial assistance related to any of these programmes. Thirdly, an annex attached to Resolution 1737 required member states to 'exercise vigilance' and to notify the Security Council if anyone named on a list of individuals and entities connected to the offending programmes was found to be on their territories, for whatever purpose. States were also called upon to freeze the assets held on their territories of any individuals or entities identified in this Annex. Resolution 1737 allowed for the suspension of these measures – thus affording space for further negotiations – provided Iran suspended all of its enrichment-related and reprocessing activities and met its UN and IAEA obligations. However, in the event that a report provided within 60 days by the Agency's director general showed Iran had not complied with Resolution 1737, the Security Council would take further steps under Article 41 of Chapter VII of the UN Charter.[10]

The Council wasted little time in taking these steps after the report indicated Iran had failed to meet a 21 February 2007 deadline for fulfilling its obligations. On 24 March 2007 it approved Resolution 1747, which reaffirmed the sanctions outlined in Resolution 1737, and imposed a ban on all arms transfers – including battle tanks, armoured combat vehicles, large-calibre artillery systems, combat aircraft, attack helicopters, warships, missiles or missile systems both into and out of Iran. Tightening the restrictions outlined in Resolution 1737, Resolution 1747 prohibited all states from providing Iran with any technical or financial assistance related to the transfer of such items. It also included an annex containing the names of a further 28 individuals or entities – with links to Iran's nuclear and/or ballistic-missile programmes – whose assets were to be frozen. Most notable about this list was the inclusion of a major Iranian bank – Bank Sepah – as well as entities and individuals of the Iranian Revolutionary Guard Corps. The terms relating to the suspension and termination of these measures remained similar to those outlined in UNSCR 1737. Likewise, Resolution 1747 called for another report within 60 days from the IAEA director general and threatened to impose further measures if Iranian compliance with both resolutions was not forthcoming.[11]

Despite the report's finding of continued non-compliance with the requirements of Resolutions 1737 and 1747, the drive towards a third round of UN sanctions was slowed by two developments. The first involved the establishment of a 'work plan' between Iran and the IAEA in August 2007, in which the former agreed to provide the latter – over a three-month period – with concrete responses to several unanswered questions regarding its previous nuclear activities. Secondly, and much more dramatically, in November 2007 the US National Intelligence Estimate (NIE) – a document produced by the 16 agencies which comprise the US intelligence community – contained an assessment that Iran had halted its nuclear programme in 2003.[12] While the NIE also expressed the view that Iran continued to retain the option of developing nuclear weapons, this seemingly startling revelation was expected to take the wind out of any further attempts to impose additional sanctions against Iran through the UN.

However, after Iran reportedly began testing more advanced centrifuges, in what was viewed as further provocation, the UN passed a third Resolution on 3 March 2008. Of particular significance was that fact that this new measure, UNSCR 1803, was passed almost unanimously, with Indonesia being the only abstainer and all other 14 UNSC members voting in favour. In the following ways, this new resolution added to the sanctions contained in the previous resolutions. Firstly, it called upon members to 'exercise vigilance' in terms of entering new agreements to provide Iran with financial support – in the form of export credits, guarantees or insurance – which may contribute to the proliferation of sensitive nuclear technologies or the development of nuclear-weapon delivery systems. Resolution 1803 also singled out an additional two major Iranian banks – Bank Melli and Bank Saderat – calling upon all states to once again 'exercise vigilance' over the activities of these institutions on their territories. A further 25 individuals – whose assets were to be frozen and international movements monitored – were identified in two separate annexes. Finally, Resolution 1803 called upon all states – within the bounds of international and their own national legal requirements – to inspect the cargoes of aircraft and shipping vessels travelling to and from Iran, provided reasonable grounds existed to suspect that those were carrying goods prohibited by this and the two previous UNSC resolutions. Member states were to report to the UNSC within 60 days outlining the steps they had taken to implement Resolution 1803 and a further report from the IAEA director general regarding Iranian compliance would follow within 90 days of the resolution's adoption.[13]

US sanctions

The US is the only member of the UNSC which has consistently sought to impose sanctions against Iran via this route. Given the amount of time – most notably in the case of Resolution 1803 – it has taken to build the requisite level of support to introduce new sanctions through the UN, however, Washington has experienced a degree of frustration with the slow pace of progress. As this section goes on to detail, the US has since 2005 unilaterally applied targeted financial sanctions, which in substance have both 'got out in front' of UNSC measures in terms of the timing of their introduction and also 'gone beyond' those sanctions imposed through the UN in terms of their substance.

The history of unilateral American sanctions against Iran is, of course, a long one which can be dated back to the hostage crisis of 1979. In direct response to the seizing of the US Embassy in Tehran, President Jimmy Carter imposed a freeze on $12 billion worth of Iranian assets and a temporary ban on all American imports from Iran. The following year, with the hostage crisis unresolved, Carter imposed further sanctions on all travel and commerce between the US and Iran. Throughout the 1980s, Iran's support for terrorist activities led to further American sanctions being imposed against it. In 1984, for example, the US designated Iran as a sponsor of terrorism and placed a ban on most forms of American economic assistance – including US support for loans and aid through international financial institutions – and arms-related exports. Further controls were also placed on the export of dual-use items from the US. In 1987, President Ronald Reagan subsequently applied a ban on all US imports from Iran in response to Tehran's ongoing support for terrorist activities. US sanctions against Iran continued to broaden throughout the 1990s, with President Clinton imposing a blanket prohibition on virtually all US economic transactions with Iran in May 1995. Of particular significance was the introduction of the Iran–Libya Sanctions Act (ILSA) in August of the following year. This somewhat controversial piece of legislation required penalties to be imposed against foreign firms which invested more than $20 million in Iran's oil and gas industry, although a presidential waiver provision written into the legislation has meant that no such extraterritorial sanctions have yet to actually be applied.[14]

In the context of the current Iranian nuclear crisis American efforts to influence Tehran's policies through the use of sanctions were initially complicated by the fact that there were already so many US restrictions in place against Iran, addressing a vast range of different issues and areas. This, in turn, meant that trade between the two countries was next to non-existent and so too the apparent points against which the US could exert additional pressure. Accordingly, as in the North Korean case, Washington moved from mid-2005 onwards to put in place a range of targeted financial sanctions (enacted under Executive Order 13382) that sought to deny Iran's access to the international business sector by exploiting the advantages deriving from America's position as the world's leading financial centre. In terms of process, while the US Department of State continued to drive Washington's efforts to apply sanctions via the UNSC route, the US Treasury Department took the lead in implementing this new, more targeted sanctions strategy.

The new approach essentially had two targets. The first was Iranian entities and individuals with links to Iran's nuclear and/or ballistic-missile programmes, as well as those who had been supportive of Iran's terrorist-related activities. US financial sanctions were designed to freeze the American-based assets of these individuals and entities and to prohibit them from doing business with their American counterparts. The express purpose of these measures was to shut the Iranian entities and individuals in question off from the US financial system. Even prior to mid-2005, the US had certainly targeted foreign entities in the context of the Iranian nuclear crisis. Between 2003 and 2004, for example, the US imposed sanctions under the 2000 Iran Proliferation Act on a number of Chinese and North

Korean companies – as well as against a smaller number of firms from Belarus, Macedonia, Russia, Taiwan and the UAE – who were accused of assisting Iran's weapons programmes.[15]

The authority for the new approach, however, derived from Executive Order 13382, which came into force in June 2005 and which initially listed three Iranian entities – including the Atomic Energy Organisation of Iran – as targets of new US sanctions measures.[16] Over the following two years, the most significant applications of these new targeted measures were against major Iranian banks. In September 2006, for instance, Iran's Bank Saderat was the first such Iranian bank to be subjected to US 'smart sanctions', followed by Bank Sepah in January 2007. Iran's largest bank, Bank Melli, was then added to the list in October 2007, along with Bank Melat and, equally significantly, the International Quds Force Unit of Iran's Revolutionary Guard. Although the latter was an elite unit whose primary function was to conduct foreign operations, approximately 30% of its operations were business-related and it was estimated at the time to be generating an annual income in the vicinity of $2bn.[17]

This imposition of US unilateral sanctions continued in 2008. In March of that year, Washington applied sanctions against the Bahrain-based Future Bank, two-thirds of which was owned by Bank Melli and Bank Sederat.[18] In August 2008, American sanctions were imposed against a further five Iranian entities – the Nuclear Research Center for Agriculture and Medicine; the Eshfahan Nuclear Fuel Research and Production Centre; Jabber Ibn Hayan; Safety Equipment Procurement Company; and Joza Industrial Company – on the grounds that they were either controlled by or acting on behalf of Iranian entities who were already subject to US sanctions.[19] Perhaps most significantly, this broadening of US sanctions came to include Iran's primary shipping company, the Islamic Republic of Iran

Shipping Lines, and 18 of its affiliates in September 2008. Once again, this particular application of sanctions was justified on the grounds that this company had links to groups who were already subject to UN or US sanctions and that it was actively assisting these through transporting cargo, falsifying documents and using other methods of deception to conceal its own engagement in their illicit activities.[20]

The second 'target' of the new US approach were those foreign companies, especially banks, who were supporting the Iranian economy by way of financing exports or processing dollar transactions for Iranian banks. These are particularly significant in the context of oil deals, given that such transactions are generally conducted in American dollars. Since mid-2005, the US Treasury Department has held numerous meetings with executives from these (predominantly European) companies, as well as with government officials from those countries, imploring them to cease doing business with Iran on the grounds that Tehran's nuclear and ballistic-missile programmes, its support for terrorist activities and its other illicit dealings pose a fundamental challenge to the stability and integrity of the very global financial system which underpins virtually all legitimate international business activities. Of greatest concern to these companies, Washington anticipated, was not the destabilisation of that global financial system per se, but rather the fear of losing access to the US market as a consequence of continuing to do business with Iran.

Two prominent cases were held up as examples of the possible fate awaiting companies who opted to go down that path. In 2004, even before Executive Order 13382, the US Treasury Department fined the Swiss Bank UBS $100m for the unauthorised transfer of American dollars to Iran, as well as to other countries which were also the subject of US sanctions. Likewise, in December 2005 the Treasury Department fined Dutch bank ABN Amro $80m for inadequate reporting procedures relating to transactions involving Bank Melli. Underlying the new US 'smart sanctions' approach towards Iran, therefore, was a hope that these initially unilateral sanctions would, over time, become multilateral measures as foreign banks retreated from doing business with Iran, having made the calculation that the potential benefits of so doing were substantially outweighed by the risks.

The development of this more selective US sanctioning strategy towards Iran did not prevent efforts to expand the range of American sanctions against Tehran. Indeed, for at least two reasons it would be a mistake to suggest that the Executive branch of the US government has, during the period in question, been able to exercise complete control over US sanctions policy vis-à-vis Iran. Firstly, Congressional attempts to expand the scope of the Iran-Libya Sanctions Act – which subsequently became the Iran Sanctions Act on 30 September 2006 as a consequence of Libya's improved behaviour – have intensified during the period in question. Numerous efforts have been made in both the US House of Representatives and the Senate calling for additional measures to be taken under the Iran Sanctions Act against, for instance, investment in Iran's LNG sector; official credit-guarantee agencies, financial institutions and insurers of Iran; and the sale of refined petroleum to Iran.[21] In part, there is a domestic rationale here in that this dynamic is a reflection of relatively longstanding Congressional frustration with the Executive branch for not pressing Iran more forcefully over its nuclear activities and other recalcitrant behaviour. Yet, ironically, this dynamic can also be seen as having reinforced the ability of the Executive branch to engage diplomatically with Tehran backed by the threat that sanctions will likely be imposed should those diplomatic overtures fail. As the chairman of the House Foreign Affairs Committee recently put it when introducing one such bill:

> I fully support the Administration's strategy of direct diplomatic engagement with Iran, and I have no intention of moving this bill through the legislative process in the near future... However, should engagement with Iran not yield the desired results in a reasonable period of time, we will have no choice but to press forward with additional sanctions – such as those contained in this bill – that could truly cripple the Iranian economy.[22]

Secondly, state and local governments in the US have introduced sanctions of their own. In a recent prominent example, the German engineering firm Siemens faced the threat of losing approximately $300m worth of contracts with the Los Angeles Metropolitan Transportation Authority on the grounds that it had sold equipment to the Iranian regime which was used to conduct surveillance on dissidents.[23] By far the most popular form of sanction at the state and local government level, however, has taken the form of legislation requiring state-owned public pension systems to divest from companies doing business with Iran. Those include energy companies such as Total of France, Statoil of Norway and PetroChina. Over 20 US states have thus far enacted such legislation, including California, Florida, Indiana, New Jersey and Pennsylvania.[24] Interestingly, the growing popularity of such measures slowed slightly in 2008 in the context of the global financial crisis. During the first half of that year, for instance, the Maine House of Representatives rejected a bill that would have required its state-owned retirement fund to divest from companies doing business with Iran.[25] Nevertheless, under the umbrella of a campaign dubbed 'Divest Terror', the use of sanctions at the state and local government level continues to enjoy considerable support, emanating most visibly from influential Jewish lobby groups and Iranian Americans.

EU sanctions

The use of sanctions against Iran has traditionally enjoyed much less support among European governments, where a clear preference for a 'carrots over sticks' strategy has long prevailed. In August 1996, for instance, the EU even went so far as to issue an official demarche to the Clinton administration following its signing of the Iran-Libya Sanctions Act, on the grounds that it constituted an extra-territorial application of US law. In the words of an EU statement issued at the time:

> We underlined that the EU does not believe that the Iran/Libya Act is either an appropriate or an effective means of combating international terrorism. We also told the US administration of our intention to defend our rights and interests if these are jeopardised by the Act and that we reserved the right to challenge it or any measures taken under it in the appropriate international fora.[26]

In 2001, when the US Congress opted to extend the act for a further five years, the EU issued a similar statement saying that 'as a matter both of principle and policy, the European Union has long opposed unilateral sanctions laws with extra-territorial effects'. It went on to say that such laws 'threaten the open international trading system', and that it had invoked a Blocking Statute to prevent any EU company from complying with the act.[27] This opposition to the use of sanctions was obviously driven both by commercial motivations and by the fact that the ILSA was an infringement on EU sovereignty, but it also reflected a belief that an engagement approach embodying the use of incentives provided the optimal diplomatic strategy for dealing with Tehran.

The emergence of the E-3 to negotiate a solution to the Iranian nuclear crisis aptly reflects this traditional European preference for the use of incentives over sanctions. That stance began to shift somewhat in 2005, however, as evidence began to accumulate regarding the existence of a burgeoning Iranian nuclear-weapons programme, and as the E-3 approach began to unravel in the lead-up to Iran's presidential election. By this time European frustration with Iran had essentially reached a pitch, even before Iran reneged upon the November 2004 agreement and resumed enrichment-related activity in August 2005.

The EU shift in favour of sanctions was also partly a reflection of the damage to the global non-proliferation regime which Iran's apparent nuclear drive threatened to create. In this respect, European concerns were not totally congruent with those of Washington, whose central preoccupation was the prospect of nuclear weapons belonging to a so-called 'rogue state' and potentially finding their way into the hands of a terrorist organisation. But the European change of course was also intimately tied to a bargain of sorts that was struck between the US and the EU, wherein the latter would be willing to support the use of sanctions should Iran fail to cease with its illicit nuclear activities, provided that Washington became more amenable to the offering of incentives as part of the international effort to avoid such an outcome.[28]

Indications that the Europeans were taking their end of this bargain seriously became apparent in April 2006, when a confidential EU paper was leaked to the international media outlining the range of sanctions measures that the organisation could conceivably apply in the event that Iran opted not to end its nuclear programme or, at the very least, to improve its cooperation with the UN. The paper, which was reportedly authored by staff of the EU foreign-policy chief Solana, suggested a number of potential restrictions including a crackdown on export credits, a visa ban on Iranian nuclear officials, new controls on 'dual-use' technologies, restrictions on Iranians studying these and related technologies at European universities, a formal arms embargo against Iran, and a formal termination of already stalled trade negotiations between Iran and the EU.[29] The document reportedly went on to note that the EU could apply some or all of these measures either unilaterally or in tandem with the UN Security Council, contingent upon whether or not international consensus could be forged via the UN route.

Consistent with this, the EU use of sanctions during the Iranian nuclear crisis has thus far tended to closely mirror the measures applied through the UN. Interestingly, however, Brussels not only endorsed these UN measures, it also tended to exceed them by consistently adding its own restrictions. This has been characterised by some commentators as a 'gold plating' of UN measures.[30] When on 27 February 2007 the Council of the EU adopted a 'Common Position' and implemented UNSCR 1737, for instance, it included a number of additional sanctions measures. It extended Resolution 1737 to include 'all items contained in the Nuclear Suppliers Group and the Missile Technology Control Regime lists'. Albeit using similar criteria, the EU also identified additional persons and entities that would be subject to the asset freeze required by Resolution 1737 and imposed 'restrictions on admission' to these as well as those blacklisted individuals and entities.[31] Similarly, when implementing Resolution 1747 on 23 April 2007, the EU once again went beyond the UN restrictions by imposing a more comprehensive arms embargo against Iran and by subjecting additional persons and entities to travel restrictions.[32] The EU went further still on 23 June 2008, by imposing travel restrictions and an asset freeze on an additional 14 senior Iranian officials and by freezing the assets of another 13 entities including – most notably – Iran's largest bank, Bank Melli and its subsidiaries. This move was particularly significant given the bank had operations in Hamburg, London and Paris.[33] Finally, on 7 August 2008 the EU responded to Resolution 1803 by using comparatively stronger language that called upon EU member states to 'exercise restraint in entering into new commitments for public provided financial support for trade with Iran, including the granting of export credits' and required EU countries – subject, of course, to international and their own national legal requirements – to inspect aircraft and ships travelling to and from Iran that were suspected of transporting prohibited goods.[34]

None of the above is to suggest that the Europeans have completely abandoned their traditional preference for the use of incentives in responding to the Iranian nuclear crisis, even since negotiations between the E-3 and Tehran essentially broke down in August 2005. In May of the following year, for instance, the E-3 countries reportedly drafted a proposal which included the provision of a Light Water Reactor (LWR), a fuel consortium designed to allow Iran to enrich uranium to low-grade levels in Russia and a relatively low-level security guarantee wherein the EU would 'work towards "recognition of territorial integrity" of Middle Eastern countries' in return for Iran abandoning its nuclear enrichment-related and reprocessing activities.[35] Ahmadinejad infamously responded to news of this proposal by suggesting that the package of European incentives designed to induce Iran out of the nuclear business was analogous to the trading of 'candy for gold'.[36] Nevertheless, this draft subsequently formed the basis of a proposal formally presented to Iran by Solana when he visited Tehran in June 2006, this time on behalf of the E3+3 (which included China, Russia and the US).[37] It also offered Iran the opportunity to purchase previously sanctioned aircraft parts from Boeing, which it badly needed to upgrade its aging civilian air fleet – provided that it abandoned its nuclear activities.[38]

Somewhat predictably given the nature of the bargain which had been struck between the Europeans and the Americans over how to approach the Iranian nuclear issue, Washington also continued to press for additional EU sanctions during the period in question. As the EU contemplated the implementation of UNSCR 1737 in February 2007, for instance, US officials appealed to Brussels to consider significantly broader measures targeting Iran. These appeals were ultimately rejected.[39] Prior to the passage of Resolution 1803 in early March 2008, Washington pressed the EU to impose sanctions against Bank Melli and Bank Saderat. As discussed previously, the EU went on to impose sanctions against the former and its subsidiaries in June 2008. Interestingly, however, even in its official response to Resolution 1803 the EU did not impose sanctions against Bank Saderat. This is notwithstanding the fact that, as noted previously, this institution was explicitly named in the resolution. Initially, the EU resisted taking action against either institution on the grounds that they had not been subject to UN action.[40] This rationale shifted somewhat following the adoption of Resolution 1803, with European officials claiming that Bank Saderat had been sanctioned previously by the US for its alleged links to the terrorist organisation Hizbullah, but that this particular group was not included on the EU's list of terrorist organisations. In other words, the EU sanctions imposed in June 2008 were primarily targeted at entities engaged in proliferation-related activities, which is why Bank Melli was included, but not Bank Saderat.[41]

As is to be expected in any organisation comprising 27 members, marked differences existed among these member states, which undoubtedly go some way toward explaining the nature and scope of the EU sanctions imposed against Iran. On the one hand, some EU members such as the UK and France have increasingly favoured the adoption of harsher sanctions measures in responding to the Iranian nuclear crisis. In October 2007, for instance, France reportedly put forward a proposal for the adoption of additional EU sanctions against Iran that did not contain provisions for any prerequisite UN mandate.[42] Similarly, in November of that year British Prime Minister Gordon Brown vowed that Britain would take the lead in pushing for additional EU and UN sanctions against Iran – including on investment in Iran's oil and gas industry and in the financial sector – unless Tehran altered its approach.[43] In February 2008, the UK and France were also reportedly in strong support of American efforts to impose EU sanctions against both Bank Melli and Bank Saderat.[44]

By contrast, Austria, Germany, Italy and Spain consistently exhibited reluctance to apply EU sanctions against Iran. Germany was the most vocal in terms of this opposition. In April 2006, for instance, German Foreign Minister Frank-Walter Steinmeier indicated that the EU would only consider implementing unilateral sanctions against Iran if there was a complete deadlock at the UN Security Council regarding the introduction of such measures.[45] German Chancellor Angela Merkel adopted a similar stance on November 2007, when during an interview on the eve of a meeting with President Bush at his Texas ranch she said 'the United Nations is the place where sanctions against Iran are negotiated'.[46] Consistent with this, Germany was reportedly among the group of European countries – which also included Austria and Italy – which were opposed to the aforementioned French proposal to apply unilateral EU sanctions against Iran.[47] In February 2008, Germany and Italy resisted US pressure for EU action against Bank Melli and Bank Saderat, again on the grounds that neither bank had yet been subjected to UN action.[48]

While this procedural consideration has been cited repeatedly throughout the course of the Iranian nuclear crisis as a justification for opposing additional EU sanctions, it is important here to acknowledge the role that economic considerations – and the prospect of ceding ground to Russian, Chinese and other Asian competitors – has played, particularly in framing German calculations. Germany, after all, is Iran's leading European trading partner and Iran is a major market for German industrial and technological products.

Japanese sanctions

Much like the EU, Japan has traditionally resisted the use of sanctions in its dealings with Iran. To the chagrin of the Carter administration, for instance, Japan in 1979 continued to buy significant amounts of Iranian oil at high prices at the same time as the US was seeking to exert pressure on Tehran through an oil embargo against Iran. In an effort to appease US critics, Tokyo eventually compromised on that occasion by keeping Japanese oil imports to the level they were prior to the US hostage crisis. Similarly, and again like the EU, Japan initially refused to join the US in imposing sanctions against Iran in 1995–96, although once more in a concession to its American ally Tokyo did agree to terminate yen loan developmental assistance to Iran in that particular instance.

The first indications of a shift in Tokyo's stance occurred in June 2006, when Japanese officials suggested that their country would be willing to join a US-led 'coalition of concerned countries' by freezing Iranian bank accounts in Japan.[49] In November 2006, the official Japan Bank for International Cooperation froze $10bn in financing for projects in Iran until Tehran agreed to meet international demands to cease its enrichment and reprocessing-related activities. Japan subsequently went on to become a strong supporter of each of the three Security Council resolutions containing sanctions targeting Tehran. When voting in favour of Resolution 1737, for example, Japanese officials stated that they 'appreciate the adoption of this resolution which demonstrates the resolute and concerned stance of the international community towards Iran on this issue ... Japan is strongly concerned about the current situation concerning Iran's nuclear issue, and considers it necessary to address this issue in a resolute manner.'[50]

Japan's private sector has also increased pressure against Iran through the application of what might be termed 'de facto' sanctions. The most prominent example of this form of sanction was applied by the Japanese oil-exploration company Inpex Corporation and revolved around the Azadegan oil field. Located near Iran's border with Iraq, the Azadegan site is one of the largest untapped oil fields in the Persian Gulf region, containing an estimated 26bn barrels.[51] Since late 2000, Tokyo had engaged in a series of tough negotiations to secure development rights which included the granting of two major Japanese loans to Iran – one of $3bn and the other of $1.2bn – which attracted sharp criticism from Washington. Finally, in February 2004, Tokyo announced that agreement had been reached and that Inpex Corporation (in which the Japanese government had a 36% controlling stake) would become a partner in the project – costing $2bn in total – to develop the Azadegan oil field. Subsequently in October 2006, however, Inpex reduced its stake in the venture from 75% to 10%. The most likely explanation for taking this course appears to have been diminishing political support from Tokyo as a direct consequence of the Iranian nuclear crisis, which subsequently left Inpex Corporation in the position of being unable to raise the necessary funds to undertake the project. Rumours that Chinese companies would fill the void left by this Japanese withdrawal highlighted the significance of Tokyo's step, both from a commercial and a strategic point of view. Moreover, for those policymakers in Tokyo who see oil as a strategic resource, the Azadegan decision was all the more significant given the fact that Saudi Arabia had refused to extend Japan's concession to the Khafji oil field (in the Saudi–Kuwait neutral zone) in 2000.[52]

Japanese companies in other sectors have implemented similar 'de facto' sanctions against Iran in the context of the Iranian nuclear crisis. In March 2006, for example, Japan's largest refiner Nippon Oil cut imports from Iran by 15%.[53] Japanese banks, however, were the most prominent in terms of taking such actions. In June 2007, for instance, at least three major Japanese Banks – Bank of Tokyo Mitsubishi UFJ, Mizuho, and Sumitomo Mitsui – expressed their unwillingness to grant Iran's request to pay for Japanese oil imports in a currency other than US dollars. At that time, it also emerged that these three institutions had informed Tehran the previous April that they would not be conducting any new business with Iran. These steps were significant in that they indicated a willingness on the part of Japanese financial institutions to go further than their European counterparts in applying pressure against Iran. For while the latter have certainly reduced US dollar transactions with Iran in the context of the nuclear crisis, they have also been willing to conduct such transactions in alternative currencies, namely in euros.[54]

The factors driving and shaping the Japanese use of sanctions during the Iranian nuclear crisis are numerous and complex. Foremost among these, Tokyo's concern regarding North Korea's nuclear activities and its desire that a firm stance be taken against Pyongyang has meant that, for reasons of consistency, Japan has essentially been forced to take a relatively strong stance against Iran's apparent pursuit of nuclear-weapons capabilities. As has historically been the case, pressure from Washington has also unquestionably played a role, particularly over the issue of developing the Azadegan oil field. Japan's genuine and longstanding support for the nuclear non-proliferation regime has been a contributory factor. So too have personalities, with the influence of Japanese Prime Minister Shinzo Abe reportedly playing a pivotal role in Japan's toughening posture against Iran during his tenure of September 2006-September 2007.[55]

At the same time, however, Japan's energy security situation and its longstanding dependence upon Iranian oil have also conditioned Tokyo's sanctioning strategies towards Tehran. Japan, after all, imports approximately 14% of its oil from Iran. Indeed, it is precisely this continued dependence on Iranian oil which explains why the Japanese government, in particular, has not played a leading role in terms of initiating unilateral sanctions against Iran – preferring instead to rely upon less obvious 'de facto' sanctions. George Perkovich, director of the Nuclear Policy Program at the Carnegie Endowment for International Peace, writes:

On balance, Japan will follow but not lead international policy toward Iran. Japan will join in if consensus emerges among the permanent members of the UNSC. Japanese financial institutions will join other major economic powers by disinvesting from projects with Iranian counterparts as needed to protect larger Japanese interests in US and European markets but will not take the lead in this direction. Given the facts of Iran's noncompliance with the IAEA and with legally binding UNSC resolutions, Tokyo could communicate to Tehran that Japan is merely upholding the rules of the global non-proliferation regime and UN system and that Iran's compliance would allow the two states to pursue full cooperation. In any event, Japan would not play a major role in broader regional strategies to shape Iranian behaviour, either through hard or soft containment.[56]

Chinese and Russian sanctions

The Japanese approach to sanctions against Iran contrasts sharply with that adopted by both China and Russia. Among the great powers, these two countries have been the most consistent in opposing the application of such measures against Iran. In November 2004, for instance, Chinese Foreign Minister Li Zhaoxing even went so far as to publicly declare that China would block outright any attempt to refer Iran's nuclear programme to the UN.[57] Senior Chinese officials have made similar public statements since then.[58] On those occasions where Beijing and Moscow have ultimately agreed to the use of sanctions – such as when both governments signed on to Resolutions 1737, 1747 and 1803 – their acquiescence has typically only been forthcoming following a period of protracted debate and after any proposed sanctions have been watered down considerably. Both China and Russia have generally preferred the use of incentives over sanctions in responding to the Iranian nuclear issue and have each advocated diplomacy over coercion. When opposing an initial attempt to impose a third round of sanctions through the UN in May 2007, for example, Beijing and Moscow each argued that diplomacy should be given more time.[59] As the following analysis demonstrates, however, while there are many commonalties underpinning Chinese and Russian opposition to the use of sanctions, there are also important differences, the underlying causes of which are often nuanced and complex. In Russia's case, for instance, Moscow's preference for diplomacy is in part premised on a belief that such an approach ultimately provides far greater insights into the Iranian nuclear programme than a sanctions policy that will bring the crisis – in the words of then President Vladimir Putin – 'to a dead end'.[60] China's opposition, in contrast, relates more closely to its longstanding objection to the use of sanctions as an infringement on sovereignty, stemming partly from its own negative experience of having been subjected to a broad-ranging international sanctions regime following the Tiananmen Square massacre of 4 June 1989.

China and Russia each have strong geopolitical motives for opposing the use of sanctions against Iran. Both countries, for example, regard sanctions as a potential prelude to war which could be just as destabilising, if not more profoundly so, as the March 2003 US-led invasion of Iraq. Paradoxically in this context, however, in China's case the cultivation of closer strategic relations with Tehran through such mechanisms as the Shanghai Cooperation Organisation (SCO) – and hence its reluctance to apply sanctions against Iran – is also intimately related to its larger strategy of balancing against and, indeed, directly competing with American power and presence in the Middle East.[61] Russia too wants to prevent the US from expanding its influence in Central Asia. But Russia's geopolitical considerations are also related directly to Iran's burgeoning strategic influence. Largely as a consequence of the Iraq War, Iran has emerged as the dominant power in the Middle East. It is a country with the capacity to project power not only into the Persian Gulf region, but also into areas which Moscow regards as lying within Russia's sphere of influence –

namely the Caucuses and Central Asia. As Thomas E. Graham of the Carnegie Endowment for International Peace observes, 'Moscow has valued Iran's decision to meddle little in Central Asia and its refusal to support the Chechen rebels or otherwise fuel instability in Russia's North Caucasus region (contrary to the thrust of US policy in those regions, from Moscow's stand-point).'[62] Russia's opposition to the use of anything but the most low-level of sanctions against Tehran thus needs to be viewed in this context.

Energy considerations also fuel both Chinese and Russian opposition to the use of sanctions against Iran. In China's case, this opposition is two-dimensional. Firstly, China is becom-ing increasingly dependent upon Iranian oil and natural gas imports to sustain its impressive economic rise and the sense of legitimacy that continued economic growth bestows upon the Chinese leadership in the eyes of many of its subjects. Iran is currently China's second-largest supplier of oil and the volume of Iranian oil exports to China continues to rise.[63] Chinese opposition to the use of sanctions against Iran is thus partly a product of the fact that Beijing is loathe to become a party to actions that may damage or destroy those energy ties. This is entirely consistent with its reluctance to press other energy-rich regimes, such as Sudan and Syria, even though these are widely regarded as objectionable by others in the international community. Second, as alluded to in the preceding discussion of Japan's approach towards the use of sanctions, Chinese energy companies have benefited immensely through filling the void left by their American, European and Japanese counterparts. The classic example here is the case of the Chinese Petroleum and Chemical Corporation (Sinopec), which in December 2007 finalised a $2bn deal to develop the Yadavaran oil field.[64] In 2009 alone, Chinese companies signed a swathe of new deals with Iran including the initiation of a project to develop the

South Pars natural gas field, as well as a $42.8bn project to build seven new oil refineries and a 1,600km trans-Iranian pipeline. Indeed, according to one recent estimate, China's state-owned oil companies have committed approximately $120bn to projects in Iran over the past five years alone.[65] This affords Tehran a high degree of leverage over Beijing and goes some way towards explaining continuing Chinese opposition to sanctions.

Energy considerations also underpin Russian opposition to the use of sanctions against Iran. Like Beijing, Moscow has an interest in ensuring that its companies have the front-running when it comes to exploiting the lucrative commercial opportunities which exist in the Iranian energy sector. Iran, after all, currently has the second-largest gas reserves in the world and is second only to Russia in this respect. It also possesses the world's third-largest oil reserves. Just as Moscow seeks to exploit these cooperative opportunities, however, it is also well aware that Iran constitutes a major potential competitor to Russia in the European oil and gas market. Approximately 80% of Russian oil exports and almost 100% of its gas exports go to Europe. This not only provides much needed revenue for the deeply troubled Russian economy, but also affords Moscow a significant degree of leverage in Europe. This is particularly so with respect to many Eastern European countries, which are presently highly dependent upon Russian energy.[66]

This fact alone explains why Moscow has remained willing to support some UN sanctions against Iran and has periodically entertained the notion of imposing additional measures against that country.[67] For the longer tensions between Tehran and the West persist – and the longer it takes for Iran to develop it energy resources – the harder it will be for Iran to initiate deeper energy ties with the European market and the easier it will be for Russia to reinforce its commercial and political foothold in that part of the world.

It is often assumed that trade considerations are also an important driver underlying Russian opposition to the use of sanctions against Iran. In reality, however, Russia's trade ties with Iran are not as significant as is often thought. According to one recent estimate, for instance, annual bilateral trade between the two countries amounts to less than $3bn, meaning that Russia does not even make the list of Iran's top ten trading partners.[68] The two obvious exceptions are arms sales and nuclear energy. As Graham observes, 'Iran is now Russia's third-largest arms market (after China and India), and one of the few countries in which Russia is building nuclear reactors.'[69] Once again, ongoing tensions between Iran and the West benefit Russian trade in each of these areas. On the one hand, they necessitate continuing arms purchases on the part of Iran. Likewise, they force Tehran to rely upon Russian technology in the nuclear sector, whereas it otherwise might seek to procure this from Western sources. This consideration too has conditioned Russia's willingness to apply sanctions against Iran. In December 2006 during negotiations leading to the imposition of the first round of Security Council measures against Iran, for instance, Moscow insisted that Resolution 1737 refer only to 'proliferation sensitive' materials in order to allow its somewhat less sensitive nuclear cooperation with Tehran (assistance in constructing Iran's Bushehr reactor) to continue uninterrupted.[70]

In the case of China, however, trade considerations are an infinitely more influential driver of its sanctioning strategies. Once again, there are a number of dimensions underpinning Beijing's opposition to the use of these measures. Like Moscow, Beijing sees commercial opportunities in avoiding the application of sanctions against Iran. In the face of Western pressure over its nuclear programme, for instance, Tehran has diverted a growing portion of its trade towards China. Reflecting the burgeoning trading relationship between the two countries, for instance, two-way trade between China and Iran increased by 35% in 2008 alone, to reach $27bn. Moreover, there are now in excess of 100 Chinese companies operating within Iran, mostly on infrastructure projects.[71] Beijing's opposition to the use of sanctions in the context of the Iranian nuclear crisis stems also from the fact that Chinese companies have frequently been the target of such measures. When the US imposed sanctions against six Chinese companies in December 2005 on the grounds that they were supplying military equipment and technology to Iran, for instance, the Chinese government issued a statement expressing its 'strong dissatisfaction with and firm opposition to these measures'.[72] Similarly, in June 2006 when the US moved to freeze the assets of four Chinese firms – including the prominent China Great Wall Industry Corporation – over their alleged complicity in providing Iran with prohibited dual-use items, the Chinese government once again issued a statement describing these measures as 'groundless' and 'extremely irresponsible'.[73]

On those rare occasions where Beijing and Moscow have been willing – albeit in a highly circumscribed manner – to support the use of sanctions against Iran, they have never done so unconditionally. Instead, in classic displays of old-fashioned 'linkage politics', they have each sought to tie their support for sanctions to the accrual of political capital and to the exercise of leverage with the US. From Moscow's perspective, for instance, the use of sanctions in the Iranian nuclear crisis is viewed as a 'bargaining chip' which can be played to negotiate favourable outcomes for Russia in the context of its larger strategic relationship with America and with the West more generally. As *New York Times* Moscow bureau chief Clifford J. Levy recently observed:

What is clear is that Russia considers sanctions as not solely an Iranian issue, but one of several that revolve around its dealings with Washington. It is negotiating a treaty to reduce the size of strategic nuclear forces, and remains alarmed by the possible expansion of NATO into former Soviet Republics like Ukraine and Georgia. If those issues are handled to the Kremlin's liking, then it will be more apt to agree to stiff sanctions.'[74]

Likewise, Beijing's support for sanctions can be viewed as part of a larger Chinese effort to project an image of great-power 'responsibility' in the international system. China's support for sanctions bolsters that image by providing a practical demonstration of Beijing's commitment to global non-proliferation norms, just as Beijing's opposition to the introduction of sanctions targeting Tehran measures may be seen as undermining that image.

Assessment and analysis

Any assessment regarding the efficacy of sanctions against Iran must necessarily begin by acknowledging that altering Tehran's nuclear policies constitutes an extraordinarily difficult task. The reasons for this are threefold. First and arguably foremost, Iran's nuclear programme enjoys a considerably broad base of support. It is regarded throughout Iranian society as bestowing an element of prestige upon the country by virtue of the technological prowess it is seen to demonstrate. More importantly, the nuclear programme is broadly regarded within Iran as an expression of 'national will' and, indeed, a right of Iran deriving from its status as a sovereign nation. Secondly, there is also a deep-seated historical rationale underpinning Iran's broad-based reluctance to abandon enrichment activities. As noted at the beginning of this chapter, Iran began a uranium enrichment programme in the mid-1980s during the Iran–Iraq War. It was a direct response to the use of chemical weapons by Saddam Hussein against Iran, stemming largely from a belief he would not have done so had Iran possessed a nuclear deterrent. Thirdly, and related to this point, the deterrent qualities of a nuclear Iran are also seen as having contemporary currency, particularly in view of the fact that Iran inhabits a strategic environment that is home to several other nuclear powers including China, India, Israel, Pakistan and Russia, and where the US – which for more than three decades now has taken an openly hostile stance towards Iran – remains deeply engaged. In this context and against the backdrop of Iran's publicly stated desire to play a regional leadership role in the Middle East, Tehran's ongoing drive to secure nuclear-weapons capability is not altogether difficult to fathom.[75] Hence, as confirmed by the September 2009 revelations of a second secret uranium facility located near the holy city of Qom, coupled with the announcement by Tehran of its intention to build another ten enrichment plants, the apparent lack of evidence to suggest that sanctions have directly influenced the decision-making calculus of the Iranian leadership is not surprising.[76] As Suzanne Maloney of the Brookings Institution recently observed:

> While Tehran is certainly capable of change, economic pressures alone have only rarely generated substantive modifications to Iranian foreign policy, particularly on issues that the leadership perceives as central to the security of the state and the perpetuation of the regime. In general, external pressure tends to encourage regime coalescence and even consolidation of its public support. Past episodes of economic constraint

have enhanced cooperation among Iran's bickering factions and increased preparedness to absorb the costs of perpetuating problematic policies.[77]

Judging the effectiveness of sanctions against Iran – particularly in terms of the traditional rationale wherein these instruments are assumed to inflict hardship upon a target actor, ultimately with a view to causing that actor to alter its behaviour – is highly problematic. This is due to the fact that economic damage that might otherwise be caused by sanctions could, in the case of Iran, actually be occasioned by that country's particular idiosyncrasies and domestic difficulties. The Iranian economy remains in a parlous state, in large part due to poor economic management. As a recent report produced under the auspices of the Economist Intelligence Unit observes:

> Economic policymaking has been haphazard for much of the post-revolutionary period. No consistent strategy towards economic development has been pursued, and the commitments of successive five-year plans to support market-oriented reforms, boost the role of the private sector and diversify the economy have not been honoured. Instead, the economy has remained dominated by the state, and heavily dependent on oil earnings as a source of foreign exchange and fiscal revenue.[78]

Most damaging has been Tehran's insistence that Iranian banks lower their interest rates to the point where it has become virtually impossible for them to generate profit. The scale of non-performing loans in Iran has also increased by an estimated 75% during the past three years alone. In terms of foreign investment, companies are increasingly deterred from investing in the Iranian oil sector due to the negligible rates of return that Tehran is willing to afford them.[79]

All of that said, there can be little doubting that the range of sanctions imposed against Iran has exacted a considerable toll on that country's economy. There is clear evidence to suggest, for instance, that a significant number of large (mostly Western) companies have scaled back their activities in Iran over recent years, primarily in response to American pressure. According to US estimates, for instance, more than 40 financial institutions have taken steps to curb their activities in Iran since the US devised its new 'smart sanctions' approach against Iran in mid-2005. Of primary concern to many of these companies is the reputational damage that can be caused to them by continuing to engage in business dealings with Iran. Oil and gas companies have at times expressed reluctance to invest in Iran given the political instability occasioned by the nuclear crisis.[80] In many cases, the tougher disclosure requirements introduced through the UN and the EU have also had a deterrent effect. As discussed earlier in this chapter, for instance, ABN Amro and UBS were fined $80m and $100m respectively for violating sanctions restrictions pertaining to Iran. More recently, the second largest bank in Switzerland, Credit Suisse, was forced to pay a record $536m fine in order to avoid prosecution for violating US financial sanctions against Iran by allegedly 'remov[ing] information from American-bound wire transfers that would have signalled that the money originated in Iranian banks'.[81]

As noted previously, while it has been predominantly Western companies that have opted to either cease or to scale back their activities with Iran in view of the above sanctions-related concerns, there is some evidence to suggest that companies beyond Europe and the US have also acted with similar considerations in mind. In early 2009, for example, Reliance Industries Ltd of India indicated that it would stop selling refined gasoline to Iran in the face of US congressional pressure on the Exim Bank of the United States to cease supporting Reliance, on the basis that those gas sales were buttressing the Iranian economy.[82] Similarly, there is also evidence to suggest that some Chinese banks have become more reluctant to deal directly with Iran and have exhibited an increasing preference for processing business through third countries, namely the United Arab Emirates.[83]

Perhaps the greatest impact that sanctions have had on Iran, however, is in terms of their capacity to engender a sense of economic and diplomatic isolation around the leadership in Tehran. Financial sanctions, for example, have created obvious inconvenience for the Iranian banking sector by increasing the time and cost associated with completing transactions. In terms of the effect which sanctions have had on Iran, however, their impact is arguably more psychological than material. The third round of sanctions imposed through the UN is often cited as indicative of this dynamic. Although the sanctions actually imposed under Resolution 1803 amounted to very little in terms of adding to the existing UN sanctions regime, the fact that support for this measure was almost unanimous (with only Indonesia abstaining) and involved governments with traditionally close ties to the Iranians (China and Russia) is widely considered to have imposed psychological costs upon Iran. Consistent with this, some analysts even go so far as to identify support for sanctions among countries that have traditionally maintained friendly relations with Tehran as a factor that has stimulated internal debate within Iran – albeit on a very limited scale – regarding the merits of persisting with the nuclear programme. As Fitzpatrick observes:

> Challenges to the government's handling of the nuclear portfolio have flared episodically in public

discourse. The first wave of open criticism came in the immediate aftermath of the passage in December 2006 of the first UN Security Council sanctions resolution, which provoked more dismay in Iran than Western policymakers had expected. The decision of its erstwhile protectors, Russia and China, to line up with the West in imposing sanctions shocked Iran.[84]

Ultimately, however, three overarching factors have acted to seriously undercut the capacity of the range of sanctions imposed against Iran to really bite. The first relates to the adaptive measures which Iran itself has been able to undertake in the face of international sanctions. Tehran has been quite effective in deepening its cooperation with other governments who are also subject to broad-ranging sanctions regimes. By way of example, it was widely reported in late 2008 that Bank Saderat had commenced negotiations with the Commercial Bank of Syria regarding the prospects for developing a joint venture which could be used to finance increased business linkages between the two countries.[85] On a much larger and more significant scale, cooperation between Iran and North Korea in the area of ballistic-missile technology is also widely known. Consistent with this, Iran continues to procure materials prohibited by sanctions on the black market.[86] Ties with the UAE have also been deepened, with many Iranian companies moving to Dubai as economic conditions within their own country deteriorate and as a means of facilitating greater levels of trade with European counterparts, many of whom are more willing to do business with companies based in the UAE. To be sure, fearing the damage to its reputation which too close an association with the Iranian regime will almost certainly occasion, the UAE has taken steps in recent times – such as tightening the inspection of cargo bound for Iran – to avoid such allegations. There have also been reports that some of the 350,000 Iranians living in the UAE have encountered difficulties renewing their visas.[87] However, given the close geographical proximity of the UAE to Iran, coupled with its need to maintain friendly relations with Iran as the dominant power in that region, there are limits to what the Federal Government of the UAE can do without damaging ties with its larger and more militarily powerful neighbour.

A second factor that undermined the potency of sanctions against Iran was the willingness of companies to step in and fill the vacuum left by those who have opted to curtail their operations with Iran. This trend has been evident across a range of sectors. As the aforementioned case of the development of the Yadavaran oil field demonstrates, it has been particularly evident in the oil industry, with Chinese companies displaying the greatest willingness and ability to secure new contracts with Iran.[88] Some Western companies have also opted not to abide by sanctions. In one of the more visible displays of their non-compliance, 450 international companies attended an April 2008 oil fair in Tehran where the biggest representations were from British, Chinese, German and Russian participants.[89] Similar trends are evident in the gas sector, where Iran has signed lucrative new deals with Chinese and Malaysian companies.

This sparked a reaction from Western companies – most famously, the Swiss trading company Elektrizitats-Gesellschaft Laufenburg, which in April 2008 signed a 25-year supply contract with Iran worth an estimated $42bn – where previously European companies had opted against signing formal supply contracts with Iran.[90] Perhaps the most consistent examples have come from the banking industry, however, where small and middle-sized banks from China, Pakistan, the Persian Gulf and other parts of Asia have been willing to fill the vacuum left by their predominantly Western counterparts. These banks do not enjoy the same level of interaction with the US financial system and are thus less apprehensive about the prospects of being excluded from it. Due to their smaller size and lesser profile, they also take a more sanguine view regarding the reputational costs which closer business ties with Iran would likely generate for their larger and more prominent counterparts.

A third factor – and that of most direct relevance to the current study – is the mediating impact of great-power politics upon the use of sanctions against Iran. Particularly so in the case of UN measures – but also with regard to sanctions imposed by the EU – the potency of sanctions has been consistently diminished because these multilateral sanctions have ultimately been the product of great-power compromise. In the case of all three Security Council sanctions resolutions the measures contained therein were more limited than what the US and the E-3 pushed for at the time. Resolution 1737, for instance, called only for states to 'exercise vigilance' vis-à-vis nuclear-related training programmes delivered to Iranian nationals, but not to prohibit them as the US and the E-3 initially envisaged. Resolution 1737 left the implementation of sanctions pertaining to the nuclear sector as a matter for individual states. The financial sanctions imposed were also considerably more limited than the US and the E-3 wanted, while the Iranian oil and gas sector were not even targeted. Moreover, the deadline for imposing these measures in the first instance was allowed to slip by almost four months before agreement upon Resolution 1737 could be reached.[91] Similarly, in the case of Resolution 1747, agreement was arrived at only after some of the more substantial measures contained in the initial draft resolution – a travel ban on Iranian officials and a termination of export credits for companies trading with Iran – were dropped. In both of these cases, the dilution of sanctions measures was a direct result of Chinese and Russian objections and was ultimately the price to be paid for their agreement to sign on to the measures in question. As discussed earlier, differences within the 27-member European Union also played an important role in terms of shaping the nature and scope of that organisation's sanctions against Iran.

A large part of the difficulty in securing great-power agreement on the use of sanctions against Iran stems from the fact that the governments in question have tended to perceive the utility of these instruments of statecraft quite differently, applying them in noticeably distinct ways and in the service of often quite disparate ends. In the case of the US, for example, policymakers operate under the assumption that it is the *actual* use of sanctions that matters and that, if applied correctly, these tools have the potential to perform the *instrumental* function of influencing the decision-making calculus in Tehran. This apparent faith in the instrumental utility of sanctions is reflected in Washington's increasing resort to 'smart sanctions' – largely targeting the access of Iranian banks to the US financial system, as well as the assets of senior figures in the Iranian leadership and their affiliates – which plays to America's strength as the world's leading financial centre.

Each of the other great powers, however, has employed sanctions quite differently and often in the service of quite distinct policy goals. The EU has traditionally favoured the use of 'carrots' over 'sticks' and seems also to have placed more weight upon the *threat* of sanctions as a way to influence Iran, rather than the actual imposition of these measures. While the Europeans have certainly exhibited a greater willingness to employ unilateral sanctions against Iran over recent years, the EU preference for the use of incentives over sanctions has lingered. Tokyo too was traditionally opposed the use of sanctions against Iran, largely due to a longstanding reliance upon

Iranian oil. In the context of the Iranian nuclear crisis, therefore, Japan has tended to favour the use of what might be termed 'de facto' sanctions whereby companies (which are often part-owned by the Japanese government) can impose restrictions on Iran, thereby demonstrating Japan's ongoing commitment to the nuclear non-proliferation regime, while at the same time justifying these measures as the product of purely commercial decisions and thereby alleviating somewhat any direct offence to the Iranian regime.

While, like the EU, China favours the use of incentives over sanctions, its opposition to sanctions stems from a more general distaste for these instruments on the grounds that they constitute an infringement upon sovereignty. That said, even the Chinese see a place for sanctions in the context of the Iranian nuclear crisis, but only after a period of protracted debate and where sanctions are employed for the express purpose of creating forward movement in a stalled negotiation process. Russian opposition to the use of sanctions against Iran is also deep-seated. Moscow, like Beijing, favours incentives over sanctions. It views sanctions largely as a prelude to war and sees the imposition of these instruments as serving only to obscure the amount of information available to the outside world regarding the state of Iran's nuclear programme.

Consistent with the central argument of this study, however, a strong case can be made that the great powers have each used sanctions – which are ostensibly directed at Iran – to also influence one another in the pursuit of their own grand strategic objectives. The US use of sanctions in the Iranian nuclear crisis, for instance, is clearly about much more than simply shaping the decision-making calculus in Tehran. When Washington applies sanctions unilaterally against Iran it consistently does so with a view to 'getting out in front' in responding to a major international crisis. It has subsequently sought to shape the sanctioning strategies of other governments by encouraging these to sign on to similar measures as part of 'coalitions of concerned' countries and, ultimately, working to see those measures introduced in the broader UN setting. By way of example, Bank Saderat was initially the target of US financial sanctions in September 2006 and that entity was subsequently identified in March 2008 as a target for UN sanctions in Resolution 1803. Likewise, Resolution 1803 also listed Bank Melli, which was subjected to US financial restrictions in October 2007. US policymakers have certainly used sanctions as a rallying point around which to build international support for their preferred approach towards Iran. But Washington has also used these instruments as a tool for demonstrating and reinforcing its capacity for leadership at the global level – which, of course, has long been a core US grand-strategic objective.

The EU use of sanctions too has been as much about influencing Washington as it has the leadership in Tehran. As discussed earlier in this chapter, the EU shift in 2005 towards the use of sanctions in the Iranian nuclear crisis was largely the product of a bargain struck between Brussels and Washington after Iran broke the Tehran Agreement (wherein the Europeans would acquiesce to the use of sanctions provided that the Americans joined the incentives package). This would appear to explain the 'gold plating' sanctions approach of the EU, which has seen Brussels adopting stricter measures than those applied through the UN and, hence, has demonstrated to Washington that the EU is keeping to its end of the bargain in its use of sanctions. Tokyo has also had Washington in mind when employing sanctions. The Japanese decision to withdraw from the development of the Azadegan oil-field development programme, Japan's aforementioned membership of the US-led 'coalition of concerned countries' and its strong and vocal support for UN measures – as a follower rather than a leader – all suggest that the Japanese use of sanctions is, in large part, both a direct response to US pressure and a reflection of a concerted effort to see similarly robust sanctions imposed against North Korea. China has also clearly had targets other than Tehran in mind when employing sanctions. Beijing's support for sanctions against Iran can certainly been seen as part of a larger drive to be perceived as a 'responsible' great power in the international system through its support for the nuclear non-proliferation regime. Yet for China, there have almost certainly been deeper, more pragmatic geopolitical motives driving its use of sanctions against Iran. Beijing's proclivity to undercut the US-led sanctions effort by consistently seeking the dilution of these measures, for instance, can be seen not only to reflect China's growing energy dependence upon Iran. It can also be read as part of an attempt to undercut American influence in the Middle East, where a battle for influence between these two global heavyweights is currently emerging. The same can be said for Russia, but with reference as well to Central Asia. What is most interesting about those rare instances involving the Russian use of sanctions, however, is that Moscow has openly used its support for sanctions as a 'bargaining chip' designed to influence US policies in areas of central national interest and importance to Russia, such as the size of America's strategic nuclear forces and NATO expansion. In the final analysis, this is significant not only in terms of understanding and explaining the use and utility of sanctions in the context of the Iranian nuclear crisis but also in offering to shed much-needed new light on the broader sanctions debate. It is to this promising potential that the concluding chapter of this study now turns.

CONCLUSION

As the first systematic endeavour of its kind to comparatively analyse great-power sanctioning strategies in the context of two major international crises, this study has revealed much about the similarities and the differences in approach which the US, China, Japan, the EU and Russia bring to the employment of these age-old tools of statecraft. These findings also promise to shed much needed light upon the longstanding sanctions paradox – why do policymakers continue to invoke these instruments with such frequency despite their outwardly dubious utility in influencing target actor behaviour – as well as calling into question some of the fundamental assumptions underpinning the study of sanctions.

Starting with the US, the defining characteristic of American sanctioning strategies to emerge from this analysis is a clear preference for the use of targeted financial measures. The employment of these tools is favoured on the grounds that such 'smart sanctions' are more discriminate and – in theory at least – impact more directly upon the target leadership than on the general public of the country in question. More importantly, targeted financial measures also play to America's strength as the world's leading financial centre. The US displays a clear preference for the unilateral application of sanctions, which allow it to 'get out in front' and to go beyond multilateral measures – such as those applied through the UN – which require an often difficult and protracted bargaining process. The US has certainly persisted with efforts to see similar measures introduced through the UNSC or within 'coalitions of the willing' among like-minded countries – such as Japan – with a view to increasing the sense of isolation felt by the target actor, thereby imposing psychological costs upon it. Typically, however, such efforts have proven time-consuming and usually result in the introduction of significantly more diluted sanctions than those preferred by US policymakers.

A strong domestic dimension also underlies the American use of sanctions. Each of the cases studied in this book suggest that sanctions have been applied against both Pyongyang and Tehran in response to domestic criticism that particular US presidents have not adopted a sufficiently robust line in responding to the Iranian and North Korean nuclear crises. A further interesting feature of the US use of sanctions revealed in this book is Washington's willingness to employ the 'lifting' of these instruments in the service of clearly stated security objectives. All too often sanctions scholars – with the exception of a few such as Baldwin – have neglected to acknowledge the relaxation of sanctions as a distinct technique of statecraft.[1] A final distinguishing characteristic of the American use of sanctions addressed in this study is the paradoxical extent to which new US sanctions have been significantly undermined by pre-existing restrictions. During the Iranian and North Korean nuclear crises, for instance, the degree of pressure which Washington is able to exert against either Pyongyang or Tehran has been severely undermined by the fact that the US conducts very little trade with either country due to the longstanding sanctions regimes it already has in place against them.

Next to the US, Japan and the European Union have, in recent years, emerged as the most enthusiastic great-power sanctioners. Brussels and Tokyo displayed quite distinctive styles and techniques when employing these instruments. The EU, for instance, appears to have overcome its longstanding opposition to the use of sanctions midway through the first decade of the twenty-first century, largely in response to Pyongyang's and Tehran's ongoing provocations and out of a realisation that its preferred 'carrots over sticks' philosophy simply wasn't working. Since then, Brussels has become increasingly comfortable with the use of sanctions, notwithstanding internal differences regarding the employment of these instruments which, of course, is almost inevitable in any organisation comprising 27 member countries. The EU has implemented each of the key Security Council Resolutions against North Korea and Iran, as well as adding to these on occasion in an approach to sanctions which some commentators have characterised as the 'gold plating' of UN measures. As part of that 'gold plating' process, Brussels has shown a clear preference of the imposition of additional travel restrictions.

Within a relatively short period of time, Japan too appears to have overcome its longstanding reluctance towards the use of sanctions to become increasingly comfortable with applying these instruments, particularly against North Korea. Prior to 2003, self-imposed legal constraints meant that Japan was essentially only authorised to impose sanctions through the UN. A February 2004 legislative amendment, however, provided Japan with the capacity to impose sanctions unilaterally. Japan has still been a strong supporter of sanctions measures introduced through the UN. Indeed, Tokyo has moved towards playing a greater leadership role in terms of initiating sanctions measures via this route. As for the unilateral application of sanctions, the findings of this study suggest that Japan has taken quite different approaches toward the Iranian and North Korean nuclear crises. In the case of Iran, although Tokyo's stance has certainly toughened in recent years – particularly during the period since mid-2006 – for reasons largely related to its energy dependence upon Iranian oil, Japan has still retained a clear preference for sanctions imposed either through the UN or in coalition with other nations. Japan has therefore been more of a 'follower' than a 'leader' in this respect. The only Japanese measures resembling a unilateral sanction against Iran have been those 'de facto' restrictions applied through the Japanese private sector. In the case of North Korea, however, Japan has demonstrated a growing willingness to play a leadership role by introducing a number of sanctions resolutions through the UN. Tokyo has also imposed a raft of unilateral sanctions against Pyongyang during the period since amending its Foreign Exchange and Foreign Trade Control Law, including blocking Japanese remittances to North Korea, imposing a range of restrictions on North Korean shipping vessels, and applying a range of trade sanctions against the North.

China and Russia have remained somewhat unwilling to impose sanctions in the context of the Iranian and North Korean nuclear crises. This book suggests that several factors underpin their reluctance to use the full force of these instruments. Economic considerations have played an obvious role. Strategically speaking, Beijing and Moscow fear the potentially destabilising consequences of sanctions leading either to war or regime collapse. Philosophically, they each have a clear preference for the use of incentives and have consistently advocated diplomacy over coercion. Indeed, when China and Russia agreed to employ sanctions these tools have generally been viewed as means to bringing Pyongyang and Tehran back to the negotiating table. Nevertheless, they have also become increasingly comfortable with the use of sanctions, with each signing up to the key UN resolutions imposing sanctions on North Korea and Iran. That said, both have consistently sought to protect Pyongyang and Tehran by seeking the dilution of these measures as a condition of their assent, while their respective implementation of UN measures has often been patchy. A degree of interdependence has also characterised the Russian and Chinese use of sanctions, with China typically agreeing to sign up to sanctions against Iran only after Russia has done so, while Moscow tended to follow Beijing's lead in agreeing to such measures targeting North Korea. Of the two countries, China has exhibited greater willingness to impose unilateral sanctions through restricting North Korea's oil and arms supplies, as well as reportedly contemplating food sanctions against the North. This study found that the defining characteristic of these sanctions as invoked unilaterally by China was the highly discrete manner in which they have been applied.

Despite illuminating a raft of differences in the sanctioning strategies of the great powers, this book has also revealed a number of important commonalities. The first of those is the negligible influence – notwithstanding the essentially unquantifiable psychological impact which they have purportedly exerted upon the leaderships in Pyongyang and Tehran – in terms of influencing the policies and behaviour of the regimes in those countries. In this regard, the experience of sanctioning North Korea and Iran serves to epitomise the so-called sanctions paradox. Third-party support for Pyongyang and Tehran has had the biggest impact in terms of helping these countries to circumvent the worst effects of sanctions, particularly those targeting trade. Chinese companies have been the biggest benefactors in this respect, moving in to fill the vacuum which has been created through the withdrawal of their American,

European and Japanese counterparts. This was shown most visibly in the case of Iran, which in recent years has signed an increasing number of lucrative new energy contracts with Chinese companies. Likewise, although showing some willingness to periodically and discretely apply unilateral sanctions against North Korea, China has also continued to provide the North with the bulk of its food and fuel supplies, as well as the vast majority of its consumer goods. Seemingly in direct contradiction to the increasingly fashionable 'sanctions can work' school, even when so-called 'smart sanctions' designed to counteract this problem of third-party support have been employed, there is little if any evidence to suggest that these measures have had a significant impact in terms of influencing the decision-making calculus of either Pyongyang or Tehran. Aside from the concern generated in Pyongyang by the Banco Delta Asia episode, Iran and North Korea have generally proven adept at implementing adaptive measures to circumvent these more selective measures. Even if they had not been able to do so, the chances of influencing the nuclear policies of either regime through the use of sanctions are almost certain to remain exceedingly low given the critical importance of viable nuclear programmes to the continued survival of each regime. These limits to influence are further compounded in the case of Tehran, given that the Iranian nuclear programme appears to enjoy relatively broad-based domestic political support.

Aside from in the US and to a lesser extent Japan, a second commonality surrounding the great power use of sanctions in the Iranian and North Korean nuclear crises has been the almost non-existent extent to which these instruments have been invoked for domestic symbolic purposes. As the 'sanctions as symbols' school predicts, the use of these instruments has played an often important stabilising role in the context of the 'cut and thrust' of American congressional and bureaucratic politics. In the case of Japan, the use of sanctions to address the domestically volatile issue of Japanese nationals abducted by North Korea during the Cold War has had some success. Beyond this, however, there was no evidence pointing towards the use of sanctions for domestic political purposes by China, Russia or, for that matter, the member states of the EU. This is hardly surprising in the case of authoritarian China and Russia, which do not typically encounter the same pressures to invoke these instruments and are not required to observe the same level of sensitivity towards domestic political sentiment. This finding, in turn, reveals a potentially serious weakness of sanctions scholarship which has focused an inordinate amount of attention upon the analysis of cases involving the American use of these instruments, thereby creating an impression that governments invoke sanctions for domestic political reasons on a more regular basis than is actually the case.

None of this is to suggest, of course, that the 'sanctions don't work' line of thinking necessarily emerges – as it has done so often in the past – as the prevailing school of thought in the so-called 'sanctions debate'. Indeed, the primary contribution of this study has been to illustrate that sanctions scholars – by focusing their attention primarily on the utility of these age-old instruments in terms of their capacity to influence target actor behaviour and/or domestic political sentiment within the sender state – have seriously overlooked one of the most fundamental purposes which great-power policy-makers have in mind when invoking these instruments: that is, to influence one another. The US has used sanctions with a view to reinforcing its global leadership credentials by 'getting out in front' in responding unilaterally to international crises and by seeking to influence the sanctioning strategies of the other great powers in the process. Particularly in the case of the North Korean nuclear crisis, the US has also used sanctions as a vehicle for encouraging Japan to assume greater global and regional responsibilities. Simultaneously, Washington has also used sanctions for the seemingly contradictory purposes of encouraging China to seek increased global and regional influence and, at the same time, of seeking to accrue strategic advantage over its most likely great-power competitor.

China, the EU, Japan and Russia have also employed sanctions with the clear intention of influencing the US. Beijing, for instance, has supported increasingly severe UN sanctions targeting Tehran and Pyongyang with a view to building a more constructive and robust bilateral relationship with Washington, while at the same time responding to American calls that it adopt a more 'responsible' international posture commensurate with its increasingly apparent great-power status. In the context of the Iranian nuclear crisis, Brussels initially agreed to support the use of sanctions with the proviso that Washington exhibit greater openness to offering inducements in negotiations with Tehran. Russia too has employed sanctions as a bargaining chip during the Iranian nuclear crisis, trading its support for these measures for what Moscow perceives as favourable outcomes for itself in the context of its larger strategic relationship with America and with the West more generally. Tokyo's support for the use of sanctions targeting Iran has also often been a direct response to US pressure and can be viewed in the context of Japan's longstanding attempts to demonstrate its value as an American ally. In the case of the North Korean nuclear crisis, however, Tokyo's support for sanctions – as well as the entrepreneurial role it has played in initiating such measures through the UN – can be understood not only in that same alliance context, but also as part of a larger effort to demonstrate to the other great powers and, indeed, the international community more generally its capacity to take on greater global and regional leadership responsibilities.

In the final analysis, the above conclusions are by no means designed to imply that policymakers do not also use sanctions with the intention of influencing target actor behaviour or for purely symbolic purposes, as the dominant schools of thinking in the ongoing 'sanctions debate' contend. What the findings of this study do strongly suggest, however, is that the voluminous sanctions scholarship suffers from three serious deficiencies. Firstly, its heavy focus upon American and, to a lesser extent, UN episodes involving the use of sanctions means that conclusions regarding the efficacy and operation of these instruments are drawn from a rather narrow selection of cases. Basing conclusions upon such a skewed sample is problematic given that the other great powers are now employing sanctions with increasing frequency, but in a manner quite distinct from that of the US. Secondly, by neglecting to adequately consider the extent to which the invoking of sanctions is typically preceded by great-power bargaining processes, in which the key players are often seeking to influence one another as much if not sometimes more than the target actor itself, sanctions scholars have thus far failed to pay sufficient attention to the diluting effect which these mediating processes can have. Thirdly, sanctions scholars have also yet to adequately acknowledge the utility that great-power policymakers continue to derive from using these instruments of statecraft for the express purpose of influencing one another in the context of executing and advancing their respective grand-strategic objectives. This latter conclusion, in turn, offers a promising solution to the longstanding 'sanctions paradox' – why do policymakers continue to employ these instruments despite their outwardly dubious utility in influencing target actor behaviour? Thus it opens up an entirely new avenue for inquiry which sanctions scholars would do well to explore in much greater depth than they have thus far.

GLOSSARY

EU	European Union
E-3	France, Germany and the United Kingdom
IAEA	International Atomic Energy Agency
ILSA	Iran–Libya Sanctions Act
LDP	Liberal Democratic Party
LWR	Light Water Reactor
KEDO	Korean Peninsula Energy Development Organisation
NIE	National Intelligence Estimate
NPT	(Nuclear) Non-Proliferation Treaty
PSI	Proliferation Security Initiative
SCO	Shanghai Cooperation Organisation
UAE	United Arab Emirates
UNSC	United Nations Security Council

NOTES

Introduction

1 For a useful exposition of this case see Hugh White, 'Why War in Asia Remains Thinkable', *Survival*, vol. 50, no. 6, December 2008–January 2009, pp. 85–104.

2 The characterisation of the EU as a great power may seem initially contentious. To be sure, the EU does possess economic weight worthy of the description, but there is not yet any single EU foreign policy, despite the controversial appointment of Lady Catherine Ashton as Europe's first foreign minister in November 2009. That said, for the purposes of this study the EU will be described as a great power on the grounds that sanctions legislation is now largely at the EU level, rather than by individual member states. Some sanctions scholars even go so far as to suggest that the EU has developed its own 'distinct approach' towards sanctions. See, for example, Anthonius W. de Vries and Hadewych Hazelzet, 'The EU as a New Actor on the Sanctions Scene', in Peter Wallensteen and Carina Staibano (eds), *International Sanctions, Between Words and War in the Global System* (London and New York: Frank Cass, 2005), p. 95.

3 See, for example, Gary Clyde Hufbauer, Jeffrey J. Schott, Kimberly Ann Elliott and Barbara Oegg, *Economic Sanctions Reconsidered*, 3rd ed. (Washington DC: Peterson Institute for International Economics, 2007).

4 See, for example, David Cortright and George A. Lopez (eds), *The Sanctions Decade: Assessing UN Strategies in the 1990s* (Boulder, CO: Lynne Rienner, 2000).

5 See Joakim Kreutz, 'Hard Measures by a Soft Power? Sanctions Policy of the European Union 1981-2004', Bonn International Center for Conversion, paper 45, 2005; and Clara Portela, *European Union Sanctions and Foreign Policy* (London: Routledge, 2010).

6 Kim Richard Nossal, *Rain Dancing: Sanctions in Canadian and Australian Foreign Policy* (Toronto, ON: University of Toronto Press, 1994).

7 Sidney Weintraub (ed), *Economic Coercion and US Foreign Policy: Implications of Case Studies from the Johnson Administration* (Boulder, CO: Westview Press, 1982), p. x.

8   Meghan L. O'Sullivan, *Shrewd Sanctions: Statecraft and State Sponsors of Terrorism* (Washington DC: Brookings Institution Press, 2003), p. 12.

9   David A. Baldwin, *Economic Statecraft* (Princeton, NJ: Princeton University Press, 1985), p. 36.

10 See, for example, O'Sullivan, *Shrewd Sanctions: Statecraft and State Sponsors of Terrorism*, p. 12.

Chapter One

1   Thucydides, *The History of the Peloponnesian War*, trans. Richard Crawley (New York: Modern Library, 1951), pp. 78–83.

2   Woodrow Wilson, compiled with his approval by Hamilton Foley, *Woodrow Wilson's Case for the League of Nations* (Princeton, NJ: Princeton University Press, 1923), p. 71.

3   Baldwin, *Economic Statecraft*, pp. 165–74.

4   See Rose Gottemoeller, 'The Evolution of Sanctions in Practice and Theory', *Survival*, vol. 49, no. 4, Winter 2007–2008, p. 99.

5   'In Cheney's words: The Administration Case for removing Saddam Hussein', *New York Times*, 27 August 2002.

6   Johan Galtung, 'On the Effects of International Economic Sanctions: With Examples from the Case of Rhodesia', *World Politics*, vol. 19, no. 3, April 1967, p. 409.

7   *Ibid.*, pp. 411, 413.

8   See, for example, Margaret Doxey, *Economic Sanctions and International Enforcement* (London: Oxford University Press, 1971); Donald L. Losman, *International Economic Sanctions: the cases of Cuba, Israel, and Rhodesia* (Albuquerque, NM: University of New Mexico Press, 1979); Robert A. Pape, 'Why Economic Sanctions Do Not Work', *International Security*, vol. 22,

no. 2, Fall 1997, pp. 90–136; Richard N. Haass, 'Sanctioning Madness', *Foreign Affairs*, vol. 76, no. 6, November–December 1997, pp. 74–85; and Reed M. Wood, 'A Hand upon the Throat of the Nation: Economic Sanctions and State Repression, 1976–2001', *International Studies Quarterly*, vol. 52, issue 3, September 2008, pp. 489–513.

9   Galtung, 'On the Effects of International Economic Sanctions: With Examples from the Case of Rhodesia', pp. 411–12.

10 Doxey, *International Sanctions in Contemporary Perspective*, 2nd ed. (New York: St Martin's Press, 1996), p. 55.

11 For more on the duties and rights associated with great powerhood see Hedley Bull, 'The Great Irresponsibles? The United States, the Soviet Union and World Order', *International Journal*, vol. 35, no. 3, Summer 1980, pp. 437–47.

12 David Mitrany, *The Problem of International Sanctions* (London: Oxford University Press, 1925), p. 76.

13 See Gary Clyde Hufbauer and Jeffrey J. Schott, with the assistance of Kimberly Ann Elliott, *Economic Sanctions in Support of Foreign Policy Goals* (Washington, DC: Institute for International Economics, 1983).

14 See Hufbauer, Schott and Elliott, *Economic Sanctions Reconsidered: History and Current Policy* (Washington, DC:

Institute for International Economics, 1985).

15 This terminology was used most famously in T. Clifton Morgan and Valerie L. Schwebach, 'Fools Suffer Gladly: The Use of Economic Sanctions in International Crises', *International Studies Quarterly*, vol. 41, no. 1, March 1997, pp. 27–50.

16 See, for example, Jean Marc F. Blanchard and Norrin M. Ripsman, 'Asking the Right Question: *When* Do Economic Sanctions Work Best?, *Security Studies*, vol. 9, nos 1–2, Autumn 1999–Winter 2000, pp. 219–53.

17 Arne Tostensen and Beate Bull, 'Are Smart Sanctions Feasible?', *World Politics*, vol. 54, no. 3, April 2002, p. 380.

18 Gottemoeller, 'The Evolution of Sanctions in Practice and Theory', p. 109.

Chapter Two

1 Thomas Fuller and David E. Sanger, 'Officials Seek Destination of North Korean Arms', *New York Times*, 14 December 2009.

2 Peter Spiegel and Chip Cummins, 'Cargo of North Korea Materiel is Seized en route to Iran', *Wall Street Journal*, 31 August 2009.

3 Blaine Harden, 'US Refuses Conditions Put Forth by N. Korea; Pyongyang Ties Nuclear Talks to Peace Treaty, Lifting of Sanctions', *Washington Post*, 12 January 2010.

4 Choe Sang-Hun, 'N. Korea Threatens to Halt All Talks With Seoul', *New York Times*, 16 January 2010.

5 Christian Oliver, 'Net Closes on North Korea's Arms Exports', *Financial Times*, 15 December 2009.

6 Blaine Harden, 'This Time, Promises Alone May Not Feed North Korea; US Seems Determined to Hold Out Food Aid until it Sees Moves to Disarm', *Washington Post*, 19 November 2009.

7 Michael J. Mazarr, *North Korea and the Bomb: A Case Study in Nonproliferation* (New York: St Martin's Press, 1995), p. 158.

8 Marcus Noland, 'The (Non-) Impact of UN Sanctions on North Korea', *Asia Policy*, no. 7, January 2009, p. 64.

9 See, for example, Curtis H. Martin, 'The US-North Korean Agreed Framework: Incentives-based Diplomacy after the Cold War', in Steve Chan and A. Cooper Drury (eds), *Sanctions as Economic Statecraft: Theory and Practice* (New York: St Martin's Press, 2000), pp. 86–109. The term 'positive' sanction is not intended to connote any form of moral judgement. Rather, it is used to describe actual or promised rewards to a target actor. See David A. Baldwin, 'The Power of Positive Sanctions', *World Politics*, vol. 24, no. 1, October 1971, pp. 19–38.

10 United Nations Security Council Resolution 1695, Adopted by the Security Council at its 5490th meeting on 15 July 2006, http://www.un.org/News/Press/docs/2006/sc8778.doc.htm.

11 Noland, 'The (Non-) Impact of UN Sanctions on North Korea', p. 65.

12 For more on the PSI, see Mark Valencia, *The Proliferation Security Initiative:*

Making Waves in Asia, Adelphi Paper no. 376 (Abingdon: Routledge for the International Institute of Strategic Studies, 2005).

[13] United Nations Security Council Resolution 1718, Adopted by the Security Council at its 5551st meeting on 14 October 2006, http://www.un.org/News/Press/docs/2006/sc8853.doc.htm.

[14] United Nations Security Council, 'Security Council Condemns Launch by Democratic People's Republic of Korea, Agrees to Adjust Travel Ban, Assets Freeze, Arms Embargo Imposed in 2006', Press Release, New York, 13 April 2009, http://www.un.org/News/Press/docs/2009/sc9634.doc.htm.

[15] United Nations Security Council Resolution 1874, Adopted by the Security Council at its 6141st meeting on 12 June 2009, http://daccess-dds-ny.un.org/doc/UNDOC/GEN/N09/368/49/PDF/N0936849.pdf?OpenElement.

[16] Dianne E. Rennack, 'North Korea: Economic Sanctions', CRS Report for Congress, Congressional Research Service, Washington DC, 17 October 2006, p.1.

[17] Despite this lifting of sanctions, a number of US laws – such as the 1945 Export-Import Bank Act and the 1951 Trade Agreement Extension Act – remained in place and continued to condition economic engagement between the US and North Korea. For a useful overview of the American use of sanctions against North Korea see Karen Lee and Julia Choi, 'US Sanctions and Treasury Department Actions Against North Korea from 1955 to October 2007', *North Korean Review*, vol. 4, no. 1, Spring 2008, pp. 7–25.

[18] *Ibid.*, p. 9.

[19] Xinhua News Agency, 'US Beefs up Sanctions against DPRK', 1 July 2009.

[20] US Department of State, 'North Korea: Presidential Action on State Sponsor of Terrorism and Trading with the Enemy Act, Fact Sheet, Office of the Spokesman, Washington DC, 26 June 2008.

[21] Helene Cooper, 'US Declares North Korea Off Terror List', *New York Times*, 12 October 2008.

[22] See, for example, Guy Dinmore and Daniel Dombey, 'Bolton: Sanctions "Help Regime Change"', *Financial Times*, 24 October 2006.

[23] See Charles L. Pritchard, *Failed Diplomacy: The Tragic Story of How North Korea Got the Bomb* (Washington DC: Brookings Institution Press, 2007), pp. 49–56.

[24] Richard L. Armitage and Joseph S. Nye, *The US–Japan Alliance: Getting Asia Right through 2020* (Washington DC: Center for Strategic and International Studies, 2007), p. 15.

[25] Thomas J. Christensen, 'Shaping the Choices of a Rising China: Recent Lessons for the Obama Administration', *The Washington Quarterly*, vol. 32, no. 3, July 2009, p. 89.

[26] Christopher W. Hughes, 'The Political Economy of Japanese Sanctions Towards North Korea: Domestic Coalitions and International Systemic Pressures', *Pacific Affairs*, vol. 79, no. 3, Fall 2006, p. 461.

[27] David Pilling and Andrew Ward, 'Japan Emollient on North Korea Crisis', *Financial Times*, 15 March 2003.

[28] Hughes, 'The Political Economy of Japanese Sanctions Towards North Korea: Domestic Coalitions and International Systemic Pressures', pp. 461–2. At the urging of Seoul

and Washington, Japanese funding for KEDO resumed in October 2009. Tokyo removed its other sanctions in December of that year, whilst normalisation talks resumed between April 2000 and October 2001.

29 Kanako Takahara, 'Japan Lowers Hurdle for North Korea Sanctions', *Japan Times*, 20 May 2003.

30 Victor Cha, 'Happy Birthday, Mr Kim', *Comparative Connections*, vol. 6, no. 1, April 2004.

31 Associated Press, 'North Korean Ships will be Barred from Japan's Ports', *Wall Street Journal Asia*, 2 March 2005.

32 See David C. Kang and Ji-Young Lee, 'Missiles and Prime Ministers May Mark a Turning Point', *Comparative Connections*, vol. 8, no. 3, October 2006.

33 David Pilling and Anna Fifield, 'Japan Imposes Sanctions on N. Korea', *Financial Times*, 11 October 2006.

34 Xinhua News Agency, 'Japan Formally Decides on New Sanctions on DPRK', 10 April 2009.

35 'Japan plans to impose ban on exports to North Korea', *Wall Street Journal Asia*, 17 June 2009.

36 Kang and Lee, 'Seirei Ketsuzetsu (Cold Politics, Warm Economics)', *Comparative Connections*, vol. 8, no. 1, April 2006.

37 Maaike Okano-Heijmans, *Projecting Economic Power: Japan's Diplomacy towards North Korea*, Clingendael Diplomacy Papers no. 21, Netherlands Institute of International Relations 'Clingendael', February 2009, p. 23.

38 'Japan Lifts Some Sanctions as North Korea Vows Probe', *Wall Street Journal Asia*, 16 June 2008.

39 Kang and Lee, 'In a Holding Pattern with Hope on the Horizon', *Comparative Connections*, vol. 10, no. 4, Janary 2009.

40 Kang and Lee, 'Little Progress on North Korea or History Disputes', *Comparative Connections*, vol. 7, no. 2, July 2005.

41 Kang and Lee, 'Treading Water, Little Progress', *Comparative Connections*, vol. 9, no. 2, July 2007.

42 Richard J. Samuels, *Securing Japan: Tokyo's Grand Strategy and the Future of East Asia*, (Ithaca, NY: Cornell University Press, 2007), p. 63.

43 Murray Hiebert, Jay Solomon and Charles Hutzler, 'US to Put Sanctions On North Korean Trade', *Wall Street Journal Asia*, 31 March 2003.

44 *Ibid.*

45 See, for example, Joseph Kahn and David E. Sanger, 'China Rules Out Using Sanctions on North Korea', *New York Times*, 11 May 2005.

46 James Dao, 'US Planning Sanctions Against North Korea', *New York Times*, 17 February 2003.

47 Andrew Scobell, *China and North Korea: From Comrades-in-arms to Allies at Arm's Length* (Carlisle, PA: US Army War College, 2004), p. 2.

48 Dingli Shen, 'Cooperative Denuclearization toward North Korea', *The Washington Quarterly*, vol. 32, no. 4, October 2009, p. 179.

49 'North Korea: Country Profile 2008' (London: Economist Intelligence Unit, 2008), p. 20.

50 Glenn Kessler, 'China Rejected US Suggestion to Cut Off Oil to Pressure North Korea', *The Washington Post*, 7 May 2005.

51 For further reading on the range of unilateral measures that China has taken against North Korea over recent years see Christopher Twomey, 'Explaining Chinese Foreign Policy toward North Korea: Navigating between the Scylla and Charybdis of

Proliferation and Instability', *Journal of Contemporary China*, vol. 17, no. 56, August 2008, pp. 418–19.

52 Kessler, 'China Rejected US Suggestion to Cut off Oil to Pressure North Korea'.

53 See Yitzhak Shichor, 'China's Voting Behaviour in the UN Security Council', *China Brief*, vol. 6, issue 18, May 2007.

54 Beijing did permit some Chapter VII language to remain in UNSCR 1695.

55 Scott Snyder, 'Political Fallout from North Korea's Nuclear Test', *Comparative Connections*, vol. 8, no. 4, January 2007.

56 Cited in Hui Zhang, 'The North Korean Nuclear Test: The Chinese Reaction', *Bulletin of the Atomic Scientists*, 2 June 2009.

57 For a useful analysis of Chinese notions of great-power responsibility see Beverley Loke, 'Between Interest and Responsibility: Assessing China's Foreign Policy and Burgeoning Global Role', *Asian Security*, vol. 5, no. 3, 2009, pp. 195–215; For further reading on Beijing's efforts to forge a more constructive relationship with Washington by way of the North Korean nuclear issue see Bonnie S. Glaser and Wang Liang, 'North Korea: The Beginning of a China–US Partnership?', *The Washington Quarterly*, vol. 31, no. 3, Summer 2008, pp. 165–80.

58 See Zhang, 'The North Korean Nuclear Test: The Chinese Reaction'.

59 For further reading see Shi Yinhong, 'China and the North Korean nuclear issue: competing interests and Persistent Policy Dilemmas', *Korean Journal of Defense Analysis*, vol. 21, no. 1, March 2009, pp. 33–47.

60 For more on Beijing's preference for unilateral over multilateral sanctions see *ibid*.

61 'UN Sanctions on NK Won't Work: EU leader', *Korea Herald*, 13 February 2003.

62 Andrew Jack, 'Koizumi says Russia could Help Resolve Crisis', *Financial Times*, 10 January 2003.

63 Leszek Buszynski, 'Russia and the CIS in 2003: Regional Reconstruction', *Asian Survey*, vol. 44, no. 1, January–February 2004, p. 164.

64 Cited in Xinhua News Agency, 'Sanctions against DPRK to Worsen Situation – Russian FM', 27 January 2003.

65 'Council Common Position 2006/795/CFSP of 20 November 2006 Concerning Restrictive Measures against the Democratic People's Republic of Korea,', *Official Journal of the European Union*, no. L 332, 22 November 2006, p. 32.

66 Council of the European Union, 'Restrictive Measures Against the Democratic People's Republic of Korea: EU Implementation of UNSCR 1874 (2009)', Press Release, Brussels, 27 July 2009.

67 Kyodo News Service, 'EU Official Backs Japan-led Draft UN Resolution over North Korea', *BBC Monitoring Asia Pacific*, 13 July 2006, p. 1.

68 Axel Berkofsky, 'EU: On the Bench in Pyongyang', Policy Forum Online 09-019A, Nautilus Institute, 10 March 2009, http://www.nautilus.org/fora/security/09019Berkofsky.html.

69 Noland, 'The (Non-) Impact of UN Sanctions on North Korea', p. 66.

70 Xinhua News Agency, 'DPRK Money to be Transferred to Russia Bank: official', 14 June 2007. The funds were subsequently forwarded to Russia's Dalkombank, which then transferred them on to North Korea's Foreign Trade Bank on 25 June 2007. See Lee

and Choi, 'U.S. Sanctions and Treasury Department Actions against North Korea from 1955 to October 2007', p. 15.

71 James Bone and Richard Lloyd Parry, 'China and Russia Oppose West's Call for Robust Response', *The Times*, 6 April 2009.

72 Ellen Barry, 'Russia: Concern Over North Korean Missile Testing', *New York Times*, 27 August 2009.

73 Michael Richardson, 'Why Russia and China are Now Taking a Harder Line', *Straits Times*, 15 June 2009.

74 Doug Struck, 'US Signals it Won't Seek Sanctions against N. Korea; At Talks in Seoul, Pyongyang's Delegates Appeal for Unity', *Washington Post*, 23 January 2003.

75 Amy Kazmin and Andrew Ward, 'N Korea Threatens "Limitless' Retaliation – US-led Curb on Illegal Trade', *Financial Times*, 18 June 2003.

76 Martin Fackler, 'Responding to UN Sanctions, North Korea Vows to Produce Nuclear Weapons', 14 June 2009.

77 Glenn Kessler, 'White Houses Voices Concern on North Korea and Uranium', *Washington Post*, 8 January 2009.

78 Mark Fitzpatrick, 'Stopping Nuclear North Korea', *Survival*, vol. 51, no. 4, August–September 2009, p. 6.

79 Gottemoeller, 'The Evolution of Sanctions in Practice and Theory', p. 104.

80 Peter Alford, 'Australia, Japan in N Korea Cash Curb', *The Australian*, 20 September 2006.

81 See, for example, Glenn Kessler, 'N. Korea Agrees to Return to Talks: A Surprise Reversal in Nuclear Dispute', *Washington Post*, 1 November 2006.

82 David Lague, 'US Negotiator Urges North Korea to End Standoff on Financial Curbs', *New York Times*, 22 December 2006.

83 See 'North Korea: Country Report' (London: Economist Intelligence Unit, 2009), p. 6.

84 Anthony Faiola, 'Despite US Attempts, N. Korea Anything but Isolated; Regional Trade Boom Reflects Division Between Bush Priorities, Asian Interests', *Washington Post*, 12 May 2005.

85 For more on the 'signalling' functions of sanctions see Doxey, *International Sanctions in Contemporary Perspective*, p. 57.

Chapter Three

1 International Atomic Energy Agency, Board of Governors, 'Implementation of the NPT Safeguards Agreement and Relevant Provisions of Security Council Resolutions 1737 (2006), 1747 (2007), 1803 (2008) and 1835 (2008) in the Islamic Republic of Iran', 18 February 2010, p.9.

2 'Obama Says US Developing New Sanctions for Iran', *CBS News*, 9 February 2010.

3 Michel Comte, 'EU Sanctions against Iran "Days or Weeks" Away: Finland's FM', *Agence France Presse*, 12 February 2010.

4 Cited in Mark Landler, 'US Envoys Head Out on a Mission to Rally Iran's

Neighbours', *New York Times*, 13 February 2010.

5   Anna Fifield and Daniel Dombey, 'US Uses Iran Nuclear Report to Push Case for Sanctions', *Financial Times*, 19 February 2010.

6   Robert J. Samuelson, 'China's "Me First" Doctrine', *Washington Post*, 15 February 2010.

7   David Ignatius, 'Putting the Squeeze on Iran', *Washington Post*, 7 March 2010.

8   Mark Fitzpatrick, *The Iranian Nuclear Crisis: Avoiding Worst-case Outcomes*, Adelphi Paper no. 398, (Abingdon: Routledge for the International Institute for Strategic Studies, 2008), p. 14.

9   United Nations Security Council Resolution 1696, Adopted by the Security Council at its 5500th meeting on 31 July 2006, http://www.un.org/Docs/sc/unsc_resolutions06.htm.

10 United Nations Security Council, Resolution 1737, Adopted by the Security Council at its 5612th meeting on 23 December 2006, http://www.un.org/Docs/sc/unsc_resolutions06.htm.

11 United Nations Security Council, Resolution 1747, Adopted by the Security Council at its 5647th meeting on 24 March 2007, http://www.un.org/Docs/sc/unsc_resolutions07.htm.

12 National Intelligence Council, 'Iran: Nuclear Intentions and Capabilities', November 2007, http://www.dni.gov/press_releases/20071203_release.pdf.

13 United Nations Security Council, Resolution 1803, Adopted by the Security Council at its 5848th Meeting on 3 March 2008, http://www.un.org/Docs/sc/unsc_resolutions08.htm.

14 The first 'test case' for this waiver provision occurred in May 1998, when on 'national interest' grounds the Clinton administration waived the application of ILSA sanctions against a French company and its Russian and Malaysian partners who were engaged in a $2bn project to develop the South Pars gas field. In return for Clinton's exercise of this waiver, the EU committed to deepened counter-terrorism and counter-proliferation cooperation with the US. For further reading on the history of US sanctions against Iran see O'Sullivan, *Shrewd Sanctions: Statecraft and State Sponsors of Terrorism*, pp. 45–103.

15 See Sanger, 'US Penalizes 6 Asian Firms For Helping Iran Arm Itself', *New York Times*, 4 July 2003; and Freda Wan, 'US Punishes Firms for Iran Missile Exports', *South China Morning Post*, 4 April 2004.

16 The President, 'Executive Order 13382 – Blocking Property of Weapons of Mass Destruction Proliferators and Their Supporters', *Federal Register*, vol.70, no.126, 1 July 2005.

17 Daniel Dombey, Hugh Williamson and Najmeh Bozorgmehr, 'US Bypasses UN with Iran Sanctions', *Financial Times*, 25 October 2007.

18 Dombey, 'US Applies Sanctions to Third Iran Bank', *Financial Times*, 13 March 2008.

19 Reuters, 'Treasury Expands Iran Sanctions', *New York Times*, 13 August 2008.

20 Dombey, 'US Imposes Fresh Sanctions on Iran', *Financial Times*, 11 September 2008.

21 For further reading see Kenneth Katzman, *Iran Sanctions*, CRS Report for Congress, Congressional Research Service, Washington DC, 9 July 2009.

22 *Ibid*, p. 7.

23 See Eli Lake, 'Siemens Risks Losses Due to Iran ties; Los Angeles to Vote on

Transit Contracts', *Washington Times*, 17 July 2009.

24 'Money Talks against Terrorism; States Should Divest from Outlaw Regime', *The Washington Times*, 11 May 2009.

25 Craig Karmin, 'Pension Funds Gain Leeway On Terror Laws – Lawmakers Ease Stance on Divestment Push as Credit Crisis Pinches', *Wall Street Journal*, 15 April 2008.

26 Europa, 'Irish Presidency and Commission Protested to the US Administration against the Iran/Libya Sanctions Act', Press Release, 9 August 1996.

27 Statement by Commissioner for External Relations Chris Patten, 'EU Regrets Extension of US Sanctions Law against Iran and Libya', Brussels, 31 July 2001.

28 'US and EU One on Iran', *Straits Times*, 19 March 2005.

29 Dombey, 'EU Paper Outlines Tough Action on Tehran', *Financial Times*, 10 April 2006.

30 Daniel Dombey, Roula Khalaf and James Blitz, 'US Pushes EU to Shut Down Iranian Banks', *Financial Times*, 12 February 2008.

31 'Council Common Position 2007/140/ CFSP of 27 February 2007 Concerning Restrictive Measures against Iran,', *Official Journal of the European Union*, no. L 61, 28 February 2007, pp. 49–55.

32 'Council Common Position 2007/246/ CFSP of 23 April 2007 Amending Common Position 2007/140/CFSP Concerning Restrictive Measures against Iran', *Official Journal of the European Union*, no. L 106, 24 April 2007, pp. 67–75.

33 'Council Common Position 2008/479/ CFSP of 23 June 2008 Amending Common Position 2007/140/CFSP Concerning Restrictive Measures against Iran', *Official Journal of the European Union*, no. L 163, 24 June 2008, pp. 43–9.

34 'Council Common Position 2008/652/ CFSP of 7 August 2008', *Official Journal of the European Union*, no. L 213, August 2008, pp. 58–70.

35 Louis Charbonneau, 'EU Aims to Offer Iran Atomic Plants, Fuel – Diplomat', *Reuters News*, 20 May 2006.

36 Ibid.

37 The E3+3 is also referred to, usually by American commentators, as the P5+1.

38 Helene Cooper, 'US is Offering Deals on Trade To Entice Iran', *New York Times*, 6 June 2006.

39 Molly Moore, 'EU Nations to Impose Limited Sanctions on Iran; Sale of Nuclear-Related Material Banned', *Washington Post*, 13 February 2007.

40 Dombey, Khalaf and Blitz, 'US Pushes EU to Shut Down Iranian Banks'.

41 Peter Crail, 'EU Levies Sanctions on Iran', *Arms Control Today*, vol. 38, issue 6, 1 July 2008, p. 39.

42 Tony Barber, 'Respect Iran Sanctions', *Financial Times*, 12 October 2007.

43 John F. Burns, 'Britain Takes Tougher Stance on Sanctions Against Iran', *New York Times*, 13 November 2007.

44 Dombey, Khalaf and Blitz, 'US Pushes EU to Shut Down Iranian Banks'.

45 Xinhua News Agency, 'EU Proposes Limited Sanctions on Iran', 11 April 2006.

46 Najmeh Bozorgmehr, Daniel Dombey and Hugh Williamson, 'Merkel Resists Pressure for New Iran Sanctions', *Financial Times*, 8 November 2007.

47 Dombey, Khalaf and Blitz, 'US Pushes EU to Shut Down Iranian Banks'.

48 Ibid.

49 Guy Dinmore and David Pilling, 'Japan Ready to Join US in Imposing Sanctions on Iran over nuclear dispute', *Financial Times*, 24 June 2006.

50 Bruce W. Jentleson, *Sanctions Against Iran: Key Issues*, A Century Foundation Report (New York: The Century Foundation, 2007), p. 31.

51 Peter Alford, 'Japan the Sushi in Sandwich Between the US and Tehran', *The Australian*, 8 February 2006, p. 40.

52 See Yoichi Funabashi, 'Japan Mustn't Lose its Footing in Politics of Oil', *Asahi Shimbun*, 7 July 2003.

53 Government officials at the time insisted that this was a strictly commercial decision and did not represent the official position of the Japanese government. See Carola Hoyos, 'Japan Curbs Oil Imports over Nuclear Concerns', *Financial Times*, 15 March 2006.

54 Guy Dinmore, 'Japanese Banks Put Pressure on Iran', *Financial Times*, 24 June 2007.

55 *Ibid.*

56 George Perkovich, 'The Iran Nuclear Challenge: Asian Interests and US Policy Options', in Ashley J. Tellis, Mercy Kuo and Andrew Marble (eds.), *Strategic Asia 2008-09* (Seattle: The National Bureau of Asian Research, 2008), pp. 442–43.

57 Shen Dingli, 'Can Sanctions Stop Proliferation?', *The Washington Quarterly*, vol. 31, no. 3, Summer 2008, p. 63.

58 Josephine Ma, 'China Backs Push to Void Nuclear-linked Sanctions', *South China Morning Post*, 26 November 2004.

59 Cheong Suk-Wai, 'China Backs New Sanctions against Iran, Says US official', *Straits Times*, 4 December 2007.

60 Cited in Robert D. Blackwill, 'The Three Rs: Rivalry, Russia, 'Ran', *The National Interest*, issue 93, January–February 2008, p. 73.

61 Jentleson, 'Sanctions Against Iran: Key Issues', pp. 29–30.

62 Thomas E. Graham, 'The Friend of My Enemy', *The National Interest*, issue 95, May–June 2008, p. 37.

63 John Pomfret, 'Oil, Ideology Keep China From Joining Push Against Iran', *Washington Post*, 30 September 2009.

64 'China shrugs off US flak over Sinopec deal with Iran', *Wall Street Journal Asia*, 12 December 2007.

65 Pomfret, 'Oil, Ideology Keep China From Joining Push Against Iran'.

66 Graham, 'The Friend of My Enemy', p. 39.

67 In late September 2009 following revelations of a second Iranian uranium enrichment facility, for instance, Russian President Dmitry Medvedev controversially indicated that sanctions may well be imposed if other possibilities to resolve the situation were exhausted. See James Blitz and Geoff Dyer, 'Moscow Hardens stance towards Tehran', *Financial Times*, 26 September 2009.

68 Philip Pan and Karen DeYoung, 'Russia Signaling Interest in Deal on Iran, Analysts Say; Still, Obama Faces Obstacles', *Washington Post*, 18 March 2009.

69 Graham, 'The Friend of my Enemy', p. 39.

70 Mark Turner, 'Fresh drive for sanctions on Iran', *Financial Times*, 9 December 2006.

71 David Pierson, 'China's links to Iran a snag for sanctions', *Los Angeles Times*, 16 October 2009.

72 Xinhua News Agency, 'China firmly opposes US sanctions on Chinese companies', 28 December 2005.

73 Xinhua News Agency, 'China in firm opposition to US sanctions on 4 Chinese firms', 15 June 2006.

74 Clifford J. Levy, 'Warmer US-Russia Relations May Yield Little in Action

Toward Iran', *New York Times*, 28 September 2009.

75 For further discussion on the motives underpinning Iran's pursuit of a nuclear weapons capability see Fitzpatrick, *The Iranian Nuclear Crisis: Avoiding worst-case outcomes*, p. 14.

76 For further reading see Crail, 'Secret Iranian Enrichment Facility Revealed', *Arms Control Today*, vol. 39, issue 8, 1 October 2009, p. 40.

77 Suzanne Maloney, 'Sanctioning Iran: If Only It Were So Simple', *The Washington Quarterly*, vol. 33, no. 1, January 2010, p. 143.

78 'Iran: Country Profile 2008' (London: Economist Intelligence Unit, 2008), p. 20.

79 Steven Lee Myers, 'Pact With Iran On Gas Sales Is Possible, Putin Says', *New York Times*, 2 February 2007.

80 Thomas Catan and Roula Khalaf, 'Oil groups shun Iran over fears of embargo', *Financial Times*, 17 March 2006.

81 Claudio Gatti and John Eligon, 'Iranian Dealings Lead to a Fine for Credit Suisse', *New York Times*, 16 December 2009.

82 Katzman, *Iran Sanctions*, pp. 6–7.

83 Najmeh Bozorgmehr, Jamil Anderlini and Richard McGregor, 'Chinese banks put curbs on Iran', *Financial Times*, 5 December 2007.

84 Fitzpatrick, *The Iranian Nuclear Crisis: Avoiding worst-case outcomes*, p. 45.

85 Anna Fifield, Roula Khalaf and Najmeh Bozorgmehrin, 'Syria and Iran consider joint bank venture', *Financial Times*, 13 October 2008.

86 Fitzpatrick, *The Iranian Nuclear Crisis: Avoiding worst-case outcomes*, p. 30.

87 Daniel Dombey, Simeon Kerr and Roula Khalaf, 'Dubai getting message on Iran sanctions', *Financial Times*, 21 December 2007.

88 Bozorgmehr, 'Iran signs $1.7bn China oil deal', *Financial Times*, 15 January 2009.

89 Fifield, 'Fair thumbs its nose at sanctions', *Financial Times*, 17 April 2008.

90 Daniel Dombey, Anna Fifield and Haig Simonian, 'Iran-Europe gas deals anger Washington', *Financial Times*, 30 April 2008.

91 Jentleson, 'Sanctions against Iran: Key issues', p. 13.

Conclusion

1 See, for example, Baldwin, *Economic Statecraft*, p. 42.

Adelphi books are published eight times a year by Routledge Journals, an imprint of Taylor & Francis, 4 Park Square, Milton Park, Abingdon, Oxfordshire OX14 4RN, UK.

A subscription to the institution print edition, ISSN 1944-5571 , includes free access for any number of concurrent users across a local area network to the online edition, ISSN 1944-558X.

2010 Annual Adelphi Subscription Rates			
Institution	£457	$803 USD	€673
Individual	£230	$391 USD	€312
Online only	£433	$763 USD	€640

Dollar rates apply to subscribers outside Europe. Euro rates apply to all subscribers in Europe except the UK and the Republic of Ireland where the pound sterling price applies. All subscriptions are payable in advance and all rates include postage. Journals are sent by air to the USA, Canada, Mexico, India, Japan and Australasia. Subscriptions are entered on an annual basis, i.e. January to December. Payment may be made by sterling cheque, dollar cheque, international money order, National Giro, or credit card (Amex, Visa, Mastercard).

For more information, visit our website: **http://www.informaworld.com/ adelphipapers.**

For a complete and up-to-date guide to Taylor & Francis journals and books publishing programmes, and details of advertising in our journals, visit our website: **http://www.informaworld.com.**

Ordering information:
USA/Canada: Taylor & Francis Inc., Journals Department, 325 Chestnut Street, 8th Floor, Philadelphia, PA 19106, USA. **UK/Europe/Rest of World:** Routledge Journals, T&F Customer Services, T&F Informa UK Ltd., Sheepen Place, Colchester, Essex, CO3 3LP, UK.

Advertising enquiries to:
USA/Canada: The Advertising Manager, Taylor & Francis Inc., 325 Chestnut Street, 8th Floor, Philadelphia, PA 19106, USA. Tel: +1 (800) 354 1420. Fax: +1 (215) 625 2940.

UK/Europe/Rest of World: The Advertising Manager, Routledge Journals, Taylor & Francis, 4 Park Square, Milton Park, Abingdon, Oxfordshire OX14 4RN, UK. Tel: +44 (0) 20 7017 6000. Fax: +44 (0) 20 7017 6336.

The print edition of this journal is printed on ANSI conforming acid-free paper by Bell & Bain, Glasgow, UK.

1944-5571(2009)49:8;1-H